P9-BJV-202

"To read these stories by Kathy González is to know something indispensable to our lives: in every person exists a desire to be good, to do good, to be a force of positive change for themselves and others. Here is proof that the most vulnerable people, our youth, struggling in the most difficult times as teenagers, close to being given up on by others and by themselves, rise to the occasion of Great Expectations. The notice of a teacher, a counselor, an advocate working with the schools, combusts with the student's own sense of what is possible within them, a sense of seriousness that only needs attention and care to be invoked. Camp Everytown buoys and sustains our morale. What uplifting stories of success and how we need them! Out of tears, determination to endure. Out of loneliness, we see a capacity to love. Camp Everytown is a cauldron of leadership. It is an embarkation center for hope. A testament to the generous minds and hearts that see in students the possibility for lives of purpose, pride, dignity, respect, and self-respect. This is more than a healing vision. It is a dynamic vision of the heart's eyes, a way of seeing so wise that it redeems humanity. That is the larger story contained in this book, redemption, hope, and inspiration. Each story is moving; taken together, the stories in this book tell of something that is sorely needed today not just by our youth but by everybody–truly a need in every town."

– Dr. Barbara Clarke Mossberg, President Emerita Goddard College, Director and Professor of Integrated Studies, California State University Monterey Bay, Senior Scholar James McGregor Burns Academy of Leadership, University of Maryland, and Creator and Host, The Poetry Slow Down, www.krxa540.com

"Kathleen González has painted little relatable portraits of teens coming to grips with the realities of racism, sexism, and prejudice. The lessons learned in their own personal journeys can help any reader remember just how much work still needs to be done to eliminate all that divides us."

– Christi Chidester, *Benicia Herald*

A Small Candle

The Impact of Camp Everytown on our Lives

By
Kathleen Ann González

Copyright © 2009

All rights reserved, including the right of reproduction of text or images in whole or in part in any form.

González, Kathleen Ann, 1965-
A Small Candle / by Kathleen Ann González

ISBN: 978-0-9745404-9-8
First Edition
Printed in the United States of America.

Cover photo by RJ Wofford II, with the participation of Semein Abay, Andrew DeSoto, and Alicia Drake.
Cover layout and book formatting by RJ Wofford II.

Dedicated to all those
who are part of the solution

Table of Contents

Acknowledgments

Of course this book couldn't exist without two groups of people: the organization that runs Camp Everytown and the people who attend it.

First and foremost, I'd like to thank Richard Valenzuela, Camp Director, without whose leadership the camp in our area wouldn't be as powerful and transformative as it is. Richard's role in positively affecting the lives of thousands of people is immeasurable.

Along with Richard comes a host of others who coordinate and sponsor camp, most notably Clarissa Moore, our local Program Director, and Bart Charlow and Lil Silberstein, past Executive Directors of Silicon Valley FACES, (previously known as Silicon Valley Conference for Community and Justice), the organization that administrates camp, as well as Pat Mitchell, the current Executive Director, and Kate Torkaman, Executive Assistant and Program Coordinator. Furthermore, my school could not have attended camp *for free* as it has for twelve years without the generous sponsorship of the East Side Union High School District and the City of San Jose, who have contributed the lion's share of funding. Other local businesses, our district council member, and families have added to this to keep kids going to camp. Finally, the administration at Santa Teresa High School has always supported the program, allowing staff, teachers, and students to miss class in order to attend camp. Past Principal Freddie Stewart, in particular, helped our program grow beyond camp and onto our campus.

Which brings me to Michael Payne-Alex, my partner in all things Camp Everytown. During a period when I thought I couldn't spare the time to go to camp, Michael's enthusiasm spurred me on to try it, and then I was hooked. Since then, we have organized twelve trips together, and in fact we co-wrote our master's research project on its efficacy. Though Michael may not be mentioned extensively in the following stories, have no doubt that I couldn't continue my involvement in the program without his help, and the generous gift of his time and self contributes immensely to our community. My gratitude extends to his family, as well, for letting me borrow him so often.

The students and staff who attend camp inspire me time and again with their willingness to be vulnerable, take emotional risks, and share themselves with all of us who attend camp. Staff, thank you for giving of your time. Students, thank you for staying in contact with me and sharing your stories. It was your lives that inspired me to write this book, both those of you who live in these pages along with many more who also have stories to tell.

Lastly, I must thank the cadre of readers who responded to drafts of stories, helping me get past the blocks and shortcomings to make these stories what they are. Mille grazie to Usha Alexander, Danny Burbol, Renee Burbol, Christi Chidester, Tracy Langley, Jeni Lucas, Lindsay Meyers, Michael Payne-Alex, Laura Rice, Nancy Schwalen, and RJ Wofford. Of course, RJ deserves an extra helping of gratitude (with figs and stinky cheese!) for formatting the text and making it into the book you hold in your hands.

Preface

"Because of camp, I decided to work for social justice."
"At camp, I learned how to make friends."
"Experiences at camp helped me choose my college major."
"Camp made me more conscious of other people's pain."

Comments like these came to me from camp alumni, sometimes years after they had attended camp as delegates or staff. Emails would show up in my in-box, or I'd run into someone at the grocery store who extolled the virtues of camp. Santa Teresa High School, where I've been teaching English for many years, has been sending students to camp for twelve of those, and I, along with Michael Payne-Alex, have been the principal organizers and cheerleaders for the program. Corny as it may sound, I've often said that my participation in Camp Everytown is the single best thing I do as a human being, and those emails and commendations bear that out as graduates and staff continue to share examples of how their lives were positively changed by it.

They're the ones who inspired this book.

The stories contained here represent only those

culled from my high school, where I know these people the best, yet the program runs throughout Santa Clara Valley in California as well as in numerous other communities in a dozen states. I have no doubt that other schools and participants have countless powerful stories to contribute as well. However, to simplify references to camp by delegates who attended, I refer to it throughout this book as "camp."

All but one of the stories within this volume are based on interviews I conducted with participants, and though I offered them anonymity, every one of them chose to go by his or her real name. Many reiterated that they stand by who they are and value their experiences, mistakes and all. They are a brave, confident, and admirable lot. There were numerous others who were ready to share their stories as well, and I only wish I had the time to record all of them.

Though these subjects' words are accurate and true, I have fictionalized other elements of the stories. In order to bring to life each subject's story, I found that I needed to put the people back into scenes at camp that I may not have witnessed personally. Since I've attended camp nearly a dozen times, I was able to recreate realistic scenes and dialogue, and each subject has read his or her story and felt that it captures the tone and spirit of the experience. In most incidences, names of other participants have been changed, or I created other "characters" to help fill out the stories.

In a world full of racism and hate, misogyny and harassment, fear and mistrust, camp provides a light of hope. As an illustration, on the last night of camp, we sit in darkness and pass around a small candle, sharing our final thoughts and words of wisdom. Camp Director Richard Valenzuela points out that a single candle can bring light to an entire room. A single person can enlighten a group, and a single program can enrich a community. Camp has brought hope into my life and community, and my wish is that this book will help to carry the ideals of empathy, compassion, and understanding to all who are touched by the stories recounted here.

The Reluctant Hero

The altar held a few photos—a grandma, a co-worker in her grocery store apron, a smiling boy—and other mementos—a pinecone and a letter scrawled on paper torn from a notebook. In a corner of the main hall on a white table stained with markers, we kept a solitary votive candle burning in the midst of the items. We were at camp for Halloween that year, and a few people had contributed to an impromptu Dia de los Muertos altar, to commemorate the Day of the Dead and remember their loved ones who had passed on.

Making an altar is also a way for people to let go of those who are gone, producing final messages to help them move to a place of acceptance, like the letter lying at our altar. Perhaps some campers would benefit from this ritual while at camp.

Nevertheless, Romina wasn't thinking of death. As she got off the bus, she already felt impatient for things to start happening. She had her school friends, Greg and Joanne, with her; she had convinced them to come along with her to camp, feeling that they needed an intense experience in their lives.

By tradition, our counselors would wait impatiently when the bus was expected, then cheer and clap and wave to the arriving students staring out the windows. Romina noticed Robbie with his dreadlocks and Daniel, the dark emo guy from campus, and wondered about these odd-looking guys being the student counselors or Counselors-in-Training.

Counselors helped to unload the students' gear from the buses and then led them down the hill to the main hall where they got their cabin assignments. The altar was already set up; camp counselors, who had been there all day for training and team building, had already added a couple items—a stone and a drawing of a frog. "When do things get going?" Romina asked as she pulled her backpack and sleeping bag out of the pile of suitcases and baggage and followed her cabin leaders out the door. She noticed that she was the only Latina in a broad mix of brown and white skinned girls, including many juniors and seniors whom this sophomore didn't know. "I was kind of surprised to be separated from my friends," she recalls, though she had been told that one goal of camp was to create a racially diverse community.

Romina, however, was one hundred percent Mexican. Her family had arrived in the U.S. from Mexico when she was three, originally on a family tourist visa. When her mother applied for residency, the family patiently waited through many years of resident alien status, eating more white bread than before and adjusting to the heavy traffic, becoming more American with every passing year, yet still holding fast to their Mexican roots. English slipped from Romina's tongue as easily as Spanish, and she often sported a black "Hecho en Mexico" t-shirt, proud that she was "Made in Mexico."

Even though Romina had been in the U.S. for most of her life, she still retained many of the traditional mores, such as deferring to elders or not looking at an adult when she was being scolded. Like most "good Mexican girls," she knew how to be docile; in fact, her English teacher didn't think she'd even go through with the first week assignment of giving a personal speech, yet instead Romina got up and spoke clearly though quietly, sharing a painful admission about family alcoholism. Romina often apologized reflexively. When she said something funny, causing me to laugh, she then apologized for getting me off topic.

"You don't need to apologize, Romina," I chided, wanting her to stop it.

"Oh! I'm sorry!" she squeaked. She hunched up her shoulders, tipped her head downward, and smiled up from behind her dark brown hair. Hers was an endearing smile, and her dark eyes sparkled as they crinkled at the edges. Camp was going to be an adventure, she felt, but it was also an escape from her parents' marital troubles and her brother's illness. "I heard a lot of people cry here," she said. "I want to cry!" But when would the real action start?

That night, as it turned out.

Daniel had circulated among the cabins, basketball hoop, tetherball stand, and the swing set, calling students back to the main hall after their dinner break. Students arrived in groups of two and three then gathered in rows of plastic chairs, chatty but nervous, waiting for their first evening at camp to commence.

"I'm your Camp Director," explained Richard,

3

"and you are the delegates." This sixty-something silver-haired man stood before the group with a microphone in his hand, the red brick fireplace at his back. His well-worn jeans and plaid shirt looked so unassuming, and little did Romina and the others know what impact Richard's instructions and words would have on them. "We call you delegates," Richard continued, "because you represent yourself as well as others who are not here: your families, friends, classmates. What you learn here at camp, you have a responsibility to take back to others, to share your learning with them." He paused to look the campers in the eye and let his pronouncement sink in. Romina, for one, accepted Richard's charge.

"Tonight we'll be talking about racism," Richard informed the delegates. He explained some background terminology, pointing out words on his easel pad, including the escalation racism often follows from name-calling to violence and sometimes even to genocide.

Richard explained, "We'll have one group leave the room, and then you'll call out all the stereotypes and terms you've heard about that group, whether you believe them or not." He emphasized that we should get all the ugliness out into the light so we could dissect it, deal with it, then begin to purge its sting and heartache from our lives.

First, the Latinos shuffled out the back door, murmuring among themselves and wondering what they would be hearing in a few minutes. Inside, two volunteers at the front of the room wrote furiously on a large easel pad, listing all the things delegates shouted out about Mexicans and Latinos: wetbacks, beaners, lazy, dirty Mexicans, illegals, border hoppers.

Once the Latinos returned, they stood incredulously before the hateful lists. Romina knew these ideas were widely held about her ethnic group, but she recoiled at seeing them so blatantly and publicly scrawled. "This isn't right. People shouldn't say things like that," she thought. Anger and sadness vied within her as she stood with the other Latinos reading the list. Romina recalls, "It was like a nightmare. I wondered if that was how my white friends really thought about me, and now they had the opportunity to say these things."

Moreover, she didn't have this reaction only when people listed stereotypes about Latinos; instead, she found herself reacting similarly during the litany for every other group: the Caucasians, African Americans, Asian and Pacific Islanders, Middle Easterners, and gays and lesbians. Words jumped off the page. Terrorists. Gooks. Trailer trash. Bad drivers. Niggers. Welfare moms. Faggots. "I knew what kinds of things people were going to say," Romina recalls, "but I didn't know how easy it would be for them to say it." Romina's jaw hung open, and her large brown eyes grew even bigger as she sat on her hands on her orange plastic chair and listened to the recitation of stereotypes and epithets. She noticed people laughing and shouting out ideas, even her friend Greg.

"It started out as fun because it was a pretend situation," Romina remembers, "but towards the middle, people started taking on their roles more seriously. I was afraid that maybe people had been suppressing those feelings in the past, and now their real feelings were coming out." Her spirit tensed. It all felt so wrong: people's words and actions, the ease with which people stereotyped, the plethora of labels and denigrating remarks, and her realization that she had passively accepted these things for far too long. Society had accepted this behavior, and she had gone along with it.

But then it hit her: she must become an agent for change. "I'm a part of this group now," she realized as she thought of her presence at camp, "so I have a responsibility to help change things." She identified with camp and being a delegate, even on this first night, and felt that she had a responsibility to the group as well as a responsibility to her community. It was like the first domino was tipped that night, leading towards Romina becoming a change agent, albeit a reluctant one. She had spent most of her life watching things unfold around her, not acting to change them. Just how does one move from being a submissive daughter and docile student to being a leader?

Romina began stewing over this question, like tending a pot of menudo, adding thoughts and feelings like so many ingredients and spices. She visited the Dia de los Muertos altar, thinking about her ancestors and how they were defamed by the kind of comments she had seen written on the easel pad, being called wetbacks or accused of being in the U.S. illegally. They deserved better. Latinos living today deserved better. "Tolerating differences isn't enough," Romina realized. "We're more interconnected with others in this world. We need to know more about these differences and not merely acknowledge that they're there. Since we have to deal with others on a day-to-day basis, it's important to know their ways well."

By the end of the racism discussion that first night, other delegates had experienced similar transformations. Laying out all those ugly terms slapped people in the face with the hurt that words can cause, especially when the delegates saw their friends' reactions of pain, sadness, anger, and bewilderment. Like Romina, everyone was changed in some way, maybe realizing the power of words, thinking of the pain their families had gone through, or growing in empathy for all who had been hurt by prejudice. Like Richard explained, "Racism is like a wound that we need to clean out before it can heal. You have to open it up and squeeze out all the poison before the real healing can take place."

The next night's gender stereotypes discussion impacted Romina even more strongly. The men and women sat on opposite sides of the room, in rows facing each other. First, I read a series of statements for the men to react to. "Stand silently if you have ever used drugs or alcohol to hide your feelings," I directed, loath to see how many of the teenagers would rise. "Stand silently if you were afraid to show affection to another man because it would make you appear gay," I continued. And one that always made me cringe, I read, "Stand silently if you were ever hit to make you stop crying." Nearly all of the men stood. Almost invariably, they became stone-faced during this activity; actually, they were directed not to show their reactions at this time, just to simply stand or sit as witnesses to their experiences, yet it was clear that many of them struggled to mask the turmoil of emotions within themselves. The eerie quiet was punctuated only by tennis shoes on dirty linoleum or a metal chair heel scraping the floor.

Next, I sat with the women as Richard made statements about typical female experiences. "Stand silently if you ever chose not to go somewhere because you were afraid for your safety," he read, and then, "Stand silently if you've been whistled at or called a bitch or whore." His deep voice resonated. "Stand silently," he continued, "if you ever thought you weren't pretty enough." These were the kinds of questions that shone a spotlight on the choices women make or the harassment they may face daily. Many of the young women recognized their lives in these statements; they were struck by the restrictions they endured and the unreasonable expectations they allowed family, society, and men to impose on them, which brought bitter or sad tears to many of them.

Standing up as a statement was read made Romina take personal responsibility for the choices she had made. Why had she gone along with these unspoken rules about how women should act? And how would she continue to act in the future? These new thoughts were added to her simmering pot of soup.

We all sat mutely after Richard read the last statement, absorbing the impact of what we had just seen and felt. As Romina got to have that cry that she had looked forward to, she gazed across the room at the dry-eyed young men and ached for them. She was surrounded by young women shedding cathartic tears, their arms around each other's shoulders, the only sounds some soft sniffles accompanied by the whoosh of tissues being pulled from boxes. Romina sat with Joanne, patting her hair, when she looked across the room to the young men. Most of the guys had put their heads down and drew into themselves or clenched their fists and jaws. A few stared at nothing, though Romina could imagine what images their mind's eyes were recalling. Romina also noticed her friend Greg across the room, immobilized like the others, and her heart clenched again. "I always thought that girls suffered the most," Romina thought, "that guys have it easy. But because they can't show their emotions and they face so much pressure to be tough, guys have it worse. They get so much abuse. The guys aren't immune to that."

As her empathy blossomed more broadly, from feeling the effects of racism the night before to seeing the results of sexism on this night, her desire to do something increased dramatically. "I can't keep propagating these negative stereotypes," she realized. "I've got to become a leader who will not let people continue to believe that all Mexicans are uneducated or illegal or lazy."

Then the third night, cultural pride night, Romina was able to act on her new insights. She met with the Latino group and directed a skit to address stereotypes about Mexicans and Latinos. In it, a Mexican family crossed the border into California, and the daughter grew up to then celebrate her quinceañera on her fifteenth birthday. The group danced cumbias and pantomimed eating tamales and chicken mole, the delegates having so much fun at this quinceañera that it seemed like more than a mere skit. How could anyone watch them and think that the stereotype of eating a lot of beans and tortillas was a bad thing? Or that the music was annoying rather than happy? Or that having a large, crowded, loving family was a nuisance rather than a great support system?

That night a reluctant hero stepped out of the shadows. Mythology expert Joseph Campbell had identified the archetype of the reluctant hero, the idea that some heroes lie dormant until they are needed and are called upon to lead others. On that night, Romina made a promise to herself to become active in her community. She would empower Latinos to make sure that they no longer felt like they were less than what they are. "I'm going to be a powerful Latina," she declared to herself. "I want to empower others to change their community and show that we're not just a bunch of wetbacks."

Though her parents had always been proud to be Mexican, Romina learned the true value for herself, in her bones and heart. In the coming weeks and months, her reluctance sloughed away, her submissiveness disappeared, her shyness decreased—dominoes falling one by one as her self-respect grew. Romina found her place in her world. She had never before seen herself as someone who would act to change things, but that had shifted at camp. Maybe a calaca memorial skull could be added to our Dia de las Muertos altar to represent the passing of the old Romina.

Romina has made good on her promise, year after year. Back on the high school campus, she started small by convincing her friends not to use name-calling, racist remarks, and stereotypes. Next, she joined the Latino Student Union and won an office. She enrolled in the Diversity in Leadership course we offered that year, reading about how to become a leader, learning how to plan events, and discovering how to propagate anti-racist teachings, among other topics. She also returned to camp as a Counselor-in-Training or CIT, a high school student who helps facilitate discussions and lead activities at camp.

Outside school, Romina began to take part in protests and educated herself about politics. She began studying Aztec dance and became a skilled dancer, even performing on the high school campus in her glorious feathered copili headdress and full-length suede huipil dress. Later at San Jose State University, she joined a number of groups that would allow her to lead Latinos and others to find their own power, such as the Movimiento Estudiantil Chicano de Aztlan that provided leadership opportunities for high school kids. She also helped to organize Raza Day for over 350 high school students to attend workshops.

Certainly, Romina will never forget who she was, the person who started on her path to becoming a leader, a hero no matter how reluctant. Nor will she forget her ancestors and the trials they endured so she could be where she is today. She'll keep candles lit for all those aspects of her past. Even so, the new Romina is all about moving forward. Camp caused Romina to start thrusting out her chin, brushing back her hair, and raising her voice. No more apologies.

Appreciation

The tall senior with the black goatee and ponytail had one arm tied behind his back with a length of blue fabric. His clothes, too, were black, except for the red and gold script on his Korn t-shirt and the silver flashing from his earrings and the chain hanging from his studded belt. Yet despite the discomfort and awkwardness his bound arm caused, he had animated eyes and a broad smile on his face. Normally a right-handed guy, Robert used his left hand to carefully lay out a tortilla on his paper plate, scoop beans on top of it, and ladle on rice as well. He moved slowly and deliberately, caught up in doing his own thing, but passing salsa or cheese to others or accepting a handful of tortilla chips, always flashing a bright grin. Rolling the laden tortilla into a burrito was tricky, but Robert didn't complain and made the best of it. "You need help with that?" he offered when he saw his neighbor struggling.

Robert had it easier than some of the other delegates. As participants had entered the dining hall, each had drawn a slip of paper from a cardboard box, mimicking the way life randomly hands out disabilities. Counselors stood by to tie bright blue or yellow strips of cloth over a person's eyes or to bind both hands to the person's sides with yards of masking tape. While Robert tried to pour lemonade with his non-dominant hand, Hoang next to him had planted his face into the beans and cheese on his plate and was trying to scoop some up with his tongue. Catherine merely sat still, her eyes blindfolded, her hands in her lap, waiting for the experiment to be over. Camp director Richard walked behind the rows of delegates, occasionally flicking a blindfolded student on the back of the head or otherwise instigating trouble, an impish grin on his face as he scurried away. A few delegates followed his example; Nick and Diego took away Kyle's plate as he reached towards the empty place in front of him that he couldn't see. However, the majority of people helped their neighbors, spooning beans, folding tortillas, even wiping sour cream off someone's face.

For the first twenty minutes of lunchtime, delegates lived with their temporary disabilities as a small taste of what life is like for the physically disabled. While some disability simulations consist of only a blind walk, having to deal with the disability while trying to fill their rumbling stomachs added a bit of urgency and reality to this activity. "It was so real," Robert says in retrospect. "Actually using only one arm gives you a better understanding to experience it instead of just talking about it. It gave everyone the firsthand experience of the feelings people have. It's not enough just to talk about disabilities, but we got to feel what it was like."

Robert has always been a really active guy, with kinetic energy bouncing off him like sparks. Though he's normally the kind of person who rarely sits still, he approached his disability with calm, and he methodically did his best to deal with it. In fact, when Richard directed everyone to "take off" their disabilities and finish eating their lunches, Robert instead opted to put on a blindfold. "I wanted to see what it was like," he commented.

That action mirrored Robert's whole approach to camp. "When my English teacher nominated me to go to camp, I thought it was pretty cool. It was a new experience, and I always want to try new things," Robert remembers. Looking at this Mexican and Italian teen with his dark clothes, chains, long hair, and imposing height, people might expect him to be disrespectful, brooding, pessimistic, a metal-head or stoner. Yet he is the opposite. "I love difference," Robert explains. "I'm not just trying to create an image. At camp, I was relaxing, finding my inner self."

The disability simulation exercise made Robert realize he shouldn't take things for granted. "It made me appreciate what I have," he says. "People take drugs and mess their bodies up, screw up their brains. Or you could lose an eye just like that in an accident. That activity made me really see how much I have to be grateful for. I appreciate things every day." Robert admits that he had experimented with drugs for a few years, but then he looked around himself at what drugs had done to others. "I didn't want to suffer the long term effects, to be one of those people who, by the time they're in their forties, are really messed up from years of doing drugs. So I quit." He says this with a small shrug as if it's the only logical conclusion one could reach.

Once the blindfolds were off, the arms unbound, and the burritos consumed, the debriefing began. Richard handed the microphone to delegates who shared stories of frustration, anger, and empathy. "What were you feeling? What did you learn?" he asked as he circulated among the campers.

One delegate explained, "I was hungry, but first I was trying to help Melissa next to me so she had something to eat."

Another said, "I didn't want to do anything. I just waited for it to be over."

A third person shared, "I put the food on the plate and explained to Javier that it was like the hours of the clock: beans at noon, chips at three, rice at six, so he could feed himself."

"I was really pissed off," Marty said hotly, "because someone slapped the back of my head while I was blindfolded."

Richard chuckled at this mischievously. "Who would do that?" he asked, ducking his head between his shoulders, his eyes twinkling. He then explained why he had randomly flicked some students. "There are a lot of bullies out there who pick on the disabled because they can't always defend themselves very well," he explained. "I wanted you to know what that feels like."

Moving from table to table with the mike, Richard continued to hear from delegates and address other issues surrounding the disabled, such as learning or developmental disabilities or how many people with disabilities shut themselves away from others out of fear, frustration, or hopelessness. "They're often called the invisible minority," Richard explained, "because no one sees them. They stay in their homes." The suicide rate amongst the disabled is disproportionately high because many people, especially those who become disabled later in life, give up.

Richard also addressed the very common but still denigrating term "retarded" that so many people throw around carelessly and in varied contexts. The word is considered an insult now, and the prefered term is "developmentally disabled."

In fact, Robert now admits that he used to belong to that category of careless speakers. He explains, "My awareness skills got brushed up drastically at camp. Now I don't say things like 'That's so retarded' or 'That's gay.' I try to help people see how stupid it is to talk like that when it hurts people." Intuitive about people's needs and highly skilled at social interaction, Robert can help others understand the effects of their words without making them feel stupid. His laid back demeanor puts others at ease, while the passion in his eyes proves his sincerity.

Robert loved the discussions that followed each activity. "Camp touched on a lot of issues that I had thought about, but I never had anyone I could talk to about them," he describes. "I've always been someone who likes to talk about issues like racism. It made me really happy to find that there were others that I could talk to about these issues."

Not only did Robert appreciate the conversations, but also he gained an appreciation of his own strengths. On the last day of camp during the forced segregation activity, the role he played as an "isolate" gave rise to this awareness.

Robert sat alone in the corner of the main hall, hunched in a dark green chair, a bagel on his plate, and the hood of his black sweatshirt obscuring his face. His back was to the group, but the delegates all knew it was him and slid their eyes towards him in furtive glances. I recall in myself that gut-clenching feeling while looking at this usually gregarious leader silently separated from us, and I felt the loss of his presence.

All around him, students sat segregated into groups, their chairs around a table or maybe huddled into a circle. While they sat with others from their racial group, Robert sat alone. Richard made his rounds to each group, ensuring that they followed the rules of not fraternizing or looking at the other groups. Again, to instigate reactions and mimic the bullies in society, he took away one group's table and made racist remarks as he strode by. "You people are always trying to play games," he retorted as he passed the African American group.

When walking by Robert, Richard sneered, "You don't have any friends, do you?" Robert just pulled his shoulders tighter together beneath his black sweatshirt.

"I got into the role," he remembers. "If people talked to me, I got nervous."

Overall, this forced segregation activity mirrors the way society has historically separated people by race, religion, and sexual orientation. However, Robert wasn't placed with any of the groups; instead, because of his outgoing nature and ability to connect with a wide range of delegates, Robert had been chosen as an "isolate." This role was created based on the 1970s film *Cipher in the Snow* about a boy who was neglected and bullied by others until he gave up on himself and died mysteriously in the snow. Every high school campus has students like this—kids who sit alone, are teased, or are completely ignored until they become effectively invisible. This isolation can lead to poor academics, low self-esteem, dropping out, drug and alcohol use, depression, even suicide. Camp staff chose about seven delegates to play this role during the segregation activity, delegates who are deemed camp "mascots" and who will elicit sympathy but are emotionally strong enough to handle the isolation.

Robert fit the profile we wanted for the activity, but it turned out he fit the description of an isolate in other ways as well. "When I was in elementary school," Robert later explains, "I was one of those people who didn't talk to anyone. Then I changed myself a few years ago and became more social." Nevertheless, it was a weird experience for Robert to avoid talking to others for the duration of the activity, and the old feelings and memories resurfaced.

By the end of the activity, groups came back together into a large circle, ending their separation and pulling each other into hugs. Three broke away to come to Robert's side, to put a hand on his shoulder, to crouch down and make eye contact past his hood. "Come and join us," they offered, and the spell was broken.

"It was cool to see that many people kept trying, not giving up on me," Robert remembers. They were able to break through the barriers he had erected.

"That activity reminded me of how much of a waste it is not to talk to people and not be a part of the community," Robert recalls. "There's so much I can learn from talking to people. It made me appreciate that I had the strength to be outgoing."

Indeed, Robert had a lot for which to be grateful, and he had come a long way in his four years of high school, considering how he had started out. First, he had failed nearly all his freshman classes, and then he had been kicked out during his sophomore year for using a watch with a remote control device to play porn videos in class when the teacher wasn't looking. At the continuation school he was sent to, a strong and caring teacher saw the smart kid beneath the smart-ass—and told him so. Robert returned to our high school for his senior year with a determination to graduate on time. He says with satisfaction, "I went from being down a full year in credits and a straight F student to getting straight A's and being able to graduate with my class."

When I first met Robert, he was in a Mass Media class, a place usually populated with at-risk kids—disaffected, disrespectful of others as well as themselves, kids who have often given up on themselves. But within minutes of experiencing Robert's cheerful greeting, quick smile, forthright eye contact, and sincere interest in meeting me, I wondered at his placement in this class; he didn't fit the stereotype.

The $1,000 scholarship Robert won that year explained a lot. He had been nominated by a teacher and was chosen to receive the Kiwanis Club's Turnaround

Scholarship, presented to students who overcame obstacles in their lives in order to succeed in school and graduate. Robert may still look like some people's idea of a hoodlum, but reality belied that label. At the scholarship ceremony, Robert bounced with pride and beamed like a boy who just had his training wheels removed. His mother, grandmother, and aunt were all there to celebrate with him. "I was so happy that my turnaround got recognition," Robert says. "I felt proud of what I had accomplished but even more proud that other people noticed."

After experiencing the role of isolate, Robert returned to campus and made a point of talking to students who were alone. The feelings of loneliness, nervousness, and sadness were fresh for him, and he hated to see others going through that isolation. After graduation, Robert began working at a local ice creamery while taking college classes. Within months he was made manager, putting his leadership and people skills to good use. "Going to camp, I got a better understanding of how people are in the world. It's not like high school, where someone tells you, 'Don't wear that hat,' or 'Get to class.' Camp showed me that people choose how they want to act in life."

Robert had turned his life around before attending camp, but its value really lay in the validation it provided, which came at the right time to reinforce these messages. The message was, "Your gifts are valuable," and he lived that message in every interaction at camp, on campus, and after high school. "I feel proud and confident of myself," he says now. "I got it from camp."

Not Alone

Phuong sat upon the orange plastic chair, her fists balled in the pockets of her white sweatpants, rocking back and forth catatonically. She radiated anger and pain like sparks flying off forged steel. Though she sat chair-to-chair surrounded by thirty-five other young women, Phuong was clearly in her own world. I knelt beside her and asked if she were okay. All she did was respond with a blank stare and shook her head. I was afraid that if I touched her she'd shatter into tiny fragments, but without touch she might be lost completely. When I put a hand on her shoulder, she sprang from her chair and moved swiftly to the back of the room to wrap her arms around a crying Frances.

And a hero was cast.

Frances sat sobbing because she had just disclosed to us the horror of what she had been through. "I was raped—twice," she choked out, "the first time during my freshman year. I was only fourteen." Frances had gone on a date with a boy she knew, and he didn't accept her "No" when things went too far. Frances resisted, crying, but an upbringing that taught passivity worked against her, and the boy overcame her. Afterwards, all she wanted to do was try to hide the

21

truth from her family, but her sudden drop in grades and isolation from friends signaled that something was wrong. When Frances became suicidal, her family closed around her like a fist. She had been my student then, and I remembered when she had suddenly disappeared. I had heard rumors of her attempted suicide, but her father would only tell me that she was sick and hospitalized. She didn't return to school that year.

However, Frances was back at school as a sophomore, bright, energetic, taking honors classes. Her Korean upbringing pushed her to excel. It also demanded her silence.

Frances signed up for camp, which she had missed out on the previous year. She came to me to get an application, bubbling over with excitement and a smile bright with dazzling teeth and crinkled eyes. "When do we leave for camp?" she asked. "What are the cabins like? Who else is going?" I was used to Frances's many questions; she had a natural curiosity and enthusiasm for nearly any activity. Who knew what secrets that vivacity masked?

Frances's story about the rape had come out the second day of camp when she had disclosed the truth to her small group leader, Amy, who let us know what was going on. "I want to share my story with the group," Frances said, "but I don't know if I'll be able to get through it."

After Amy let me know what was going on, I had checked up on Frances myself. We stood under the cooling redwoods outside the main hall while other campers sat on the swings farther away. I held both her hands. With reddened eyes, Frances confessed, "I feel like I've never gotten the love that I deserve."

Riding her own tiger was Phuong. "I came to camp to get away from my family," she had told me the first night while we sat across from each other and crunched on salads. Her hands covered her face, and she arched back in her chair, pushing back her long, black hair. She had a classic moon-shaped face sung about in Vietnamese poems. Hands and eyes and body never still, her pain and discomfort were obvious. Phuong looked like she wanted to set up a ladder and climb right out of herself.

"My parents tell me I'm fat and ugly," she said.

Other campers sat at the long, white tables all around us, forking up pasta, laughing, quizzing the new people across from them. Here was Phuong in crisis, so alone in that crowd. How long had she been feeling this way? She and I remained at the table long after others had cleared their plates, sponged off the surfaces, and gone on to their cabins or games of ping pong. Her fears and family life spilled out until we had to join the large group for ice breaker games like "Where the Wind Blows" and "I Love my Neighbor," a lighthearted contrast to our heavy introductory conversation.

The next day, Phuong told her small discussion group leader David that on the suicide scale, she was a seven out of ten. We were all on watch and made sure she was never alone. Phuong stayed visibly tense, her neck muscles taut, and her stance rigid. Sending her home was not a safe option. Home was where the hurt was.

That night was about gender empowerment. The young men relocated out of the main hall to the staff room, while the young women scooted their chairs forward in solidarity. Two delegates stood before the easel pad, rapidly recording the messages that are thrust upon women by the media and society as fast as the women called them out.

"Women should be barefoot and pregnant," one girl pronounced.

"Women can't be president," said another.

Many of these statements brought hisses and groans or even derisive laughter. Lots of them described women's bodies, like "Women need big boobs," or "Women should have an hourglass figure." One sentence chilled me: "Women are responsible for being raped." Other comments were more enlightened, such as, "Girls can wear make up if they want, but they don't have to to be considered a woman."

"Women are strong!" yelled one strident girl, and the room erupted in hoots and cheers.

Next, the women voted. "Which of these statements would you keep? Which would you teach your daughters?" Amy asked them. The girls voted to cross off many of the negative or limiting messages about their gender. They went on to make a similar list of statements about men, later crossing off the ones that they believed were not true for a majority of men.

In their own room, the young men were making similar lists. When they returned, the whole group spent over an hour analyzing them.

"What do these lists tell us about Group A and

Group B?" Richard, the camp director, asked, omitting the gender labels in an attempt to neutralize the discussion so delegates could be more objective. Yet the tension was palpable, especially when the women saw that the men had left things on their list like, "Hit it and quit it," "Bros before ho's," and "Find 'em, feed 'em, fuck 'em, and forget 'em." Many of the girls drew closer together, sharing their disgust, while some of the boys whooped and others hung their heads.

Then it came time to stand silently and acknowledge what we'd lived through, what had been done to us. I read the statements for the men to stand up. "Men, stand silently if you've ever worked out to make yourself appear more manly. Stand silently if you listen to music that puts down women." I continued, "Men, stand silently if you've ever been hit by an older man." As many of them stood, the men showed no reaction as Richard had instructed them to do; they stared at the wall, the floor, their hands. Yet their tense faces betrayed the way society had shaped them to not show their emotions.

Next was the women's turn. Richard directed, "Women, stand silently if you ever dressed in tight or restrictive clothing to appear sexy." He also read, "Women, stand silently if you've ever said 'yes' because you were afraid of a man's anger."

Frances ran from the room out into the chilly night air.

But Amy and I brought her back and huddled with her at the side of the room. It's safer to keep everyone with the group where they have others for support. Besides, a wound can't heal if it's left full of poison and continues to fester; camp is a safe place to face the ugliness and expel it to ready ourselves to move beyond it. I whispered to Frances to breathe, and I counted aloud to help her slow down her hiccuping lungs. Frances listened, nodded, breathed more deeply. She sat back down with the other women and turned around her chair, not looking at the men, her head down. Then out of some deep place of strength, she suddenly stood and told the group that she had been raped. She told of her fear, her mistrust, her deep pain.

Phuong rocked, her whole body clenched.

I put a hand on her shoulder.

Phuong declared, "I'm tired of crying." She sprang up, took the microphone, faced the room, and told that she, too, had been raped, two years before. She had never told anyone, especially not her taciturn Vietnamese family.

Phuong strode over to Frances, ending her own victimization. Frances, in her pain and acknowledgment, may have saved Phuong's life, giving her someone to care for.

Later, after many more tears had been shed, Phuong found me. "I want to start a support group back at school for rape victims," she said. Frances stood with her, holding her hand, and a couple other girls stood behind them. Phuong's back was straight, her chin up, chest out, no longer rippling with tension but instead infused with determination.

"We can make that happen," I replied. Later, both her small group leaders and our school counselor confirmed that we didn't need to continue a suicide watch.

"Phuong is like a different person," David said, "though we've also convinced her to see a therapist to continue her healing and help her talk to her family." We counseled both girls that we'd have to file reports to Child Protective Services and that we'd be with them through the process.

After the intensity of the gender empowerment activity, delegates gathered for campfire singing before bedtime. While song leaders stood on the small planked stage and led the singing next to the boom box, delegates sat on logs or benches around the fire pit and took in the warmth, their backs to the October chill. A couple delegates brought out the posters listing stereotypes of men and women. Like wolves, the campers tore these into shreds and threw them into the fire, a sort of puja where everyone would be cleansed by fire and release the ugliness and power of those words. As the crumpled scraps burned, campers saw the words turn to ash and disappear. Phuong and Frances sat amidst a group of girls and guys, a brown plaid sleeping bag spread across their shoulders. The song leaders called out, "Next song is 'Hero,'" one of the standby favorites. Did Phuong and Frances think of themselves as they sang the lyrics?

Life's Most Valuable Privileges

"Are they going to tease me about my sexuality?" he wondered. "What will they think of me? Anthony's going to be there—is he going to harass me like he has in the past? And I have to share a cabin with eight guys—what will their reactions to me be?" These thoughts swirled through Suwai's head as he tried to ignore what the other boys were saying, comments he knew he was meant to overhear.

"Heh heh, we get to sleep in the cabins with a bunch of other guys," Anthony joked, nudging his friend Ben.

"Yeah, naked and stuff," Ben leered, glancing in Suwai's direction, as the other boys erupted in derisive laughter.

They stood in packs by their piles of sleeping bags, pillows, and duffle bags in the parking lot at the high school, waiting to board the bus that would take them to camp. Suwai stood apart from the others.

But his desire to make new friends and to find a club he could connect with was stronger than his discomfort, so Suwai looked ahead towards a positive experience at camp. Suwai had probable cause for concern. His tall, lanky frame and model's gait, his striking cheekbones, his clothes that were more fashionable than most seventeen-year-old boys, and especially his purple eye shadow set him apart from his peers. People like to look at Suwai, if not for his handsomeness then to try to discern where his polished mahogany complexion, angular features, and accent originate. And then he speaks, and his eyelids flutter, and his hands add to his expressiveness.

The bus finally arrived, and Michael herded the students aboard for the forty-five minute ride to the Santa Cruz Mountains. Delegates settled into cabins, had dinner, and played some ice breaker games before the evening's main activity. For the discussion on racism, delegates stood with the groups representing their respective racial groups; each group took its turn waiting outside while the remaining students listed terms about that group. As the Asian group shivered in the chill October night, students began questioning Suwai.

"Where are you from anyway?" asked one camper. "You don't look Chinese, or Vietnamese either."

"I'm from Burma," Suwai replied smiling. Many people had never heard of this country of fifty-four million people nestled between China and India. Or maybe they only knew the name Myanmar, the country's original name that was adopted by the military junta that had taken over the country in 1988, suspending the constitution and refusing to allow the elected officials to take their offices. Human rights violations had become common there, and Aung San Suu Kyi had emerged to fight for her people's rights, being placed under house arrest but still being recognized for her efforts with the

Nobel Peace Prize in 1991.

Suwai's family, like a million other Burmese, had fled the country for both political as well as economic reasons. Where Suwai comes from, people don't have last names, so he had had to split his one name into two parts, Su Wai, when he came to America, though he was registered at school using his grandfather's second name. After Suwai spoke at camp that evening, describing his homeland, many campers' eyes were opened, not only among the non-Asians but also within the Asian group, that category that included more than just Chinese, Vietnamese, Japanese, and Koreans. We learned about how Suwai's homeland had been terrorized by its military, and we learned that, certainly, not all Asians were short, as the presence of Suwai as well as Vietnamese Thanh also attested to, dashing another stereotype.

However, it was the night's final group that affected Suwai more strongly.

Richard directed the delegates, "Please exit the room if you or a close friend or family member identifies as gay, lesbian, bisexual, or transgendered." Participants were led out the wide, double doors to huddle together, warming each other's hands or jumping up and down for warmth. We had quite a large group that year. Inside, delegates called out all the stereotypes and epithets they had heard about this group while volunteers recorded the comments on poster paper.

"Faggots. Dykes. Sinners."

"They're perverted."

"They all have AIDS."

"They're going to rot in hell."

Once the list had filled the page, the group from outside filed back in silently. As with every racial group that had viewed lists about themselves earlier that night, the LGBT (Lesbian/Gay/Bisexual/Transgender) group stood quietly to read through the two columns that supposedly described them. Someone laughed nervously. A tentative finger pointed out an ugly term on the page. A few delegates reached for tissues to wipe away their tears. The audience was unusually quiet.

Then the standing delegates turned to face the audience and began to share their reactions. Richard peered at them from under his bushy eyebrows and prompted, "What words offend you or might offend your loved ones?"

Gino shared this story: "I'm offended by the idea that all gay people have AIDS and deserve to die. My uncle died of AIDS. He admits that he got it from unprotected sex with another man, but that doesn't mean he deserved to suffer a slow and painful death. No one deserves to go through that," he said vehemently. "And it doesn't mean that he should be treated like a freak by other people because of the mistake he made." Gino's friend slipped her arm around his shoulder in support.

"I'm a Christian," Janelle began, "and I'm offended by the idea that gays will all rot in hell. Jesus taught us to love one another. That's what my religion teaches me, not to hate."

"I'm offended by the term faggot," Suwai said. "Do you know where that word comes from? In medieval times, homosexuals were burned alive at the stake, and a faggot is literally a bundle of sticks like the kind that was set on fire beneath them."

"Have you been called a faggot?" Richard asked him.

"Yes," replied Suwai promptly. "I'm actually bisexual, but people don't know that and just assume I'm gay." He said it in such a matter-of-fact manner that it seemed this name-calling was something he had experienced so often as to make it feel normal. Suwai was able to talk about his sexual orientation with impressive self-confidence and without the sense of the shame that many people in society might try to thrust upon gays, lesbians, bisexuals, and transgendered people. Not many years ago, I never could have imagined a high school student openly self-identifying like this to his or her peers. Suwai's self-possession is partly a testament to the safe atmosphere created at camp, but it is also an example of his honesty, intelligence, and grace.

A common result of this night's activity is that campers build empathy for the pain that others have experienced due to name-calling and stereotyping. Richard asked the group, "You remember that old children's rhyme, 'Sticks and stones may break my bones but names will never hurt me'? Well, don't you believe it. The pain and the tears you saw on people's faces tonight show that names and words really do hurt, even many years later." Many heads nodded in agreement.

After that night, Anthony never again teased or harassed Suwai. The message had gotten through. He treated Suwai as a friend, chatting with him or inviting him into the circle of break dancers he hung out with.

Back in Suwai's cabin that night, the young men stayed up late, talking in the safety of "lights out." Suwai befriended a mop-headed freshman named Thomas who wasn't yet sure how he defined his sexual orientation. He was searching for identity in the high school milieu that didn't encourage open dialogue, but Suwai became a role model. "Thomas really accepted me," Suwai recalls. "We became friends right away and paired off to talk at breaks. Thomas wasn't sure if he was gay or not, so we talked about it a lot." They stayed friends after camp back on campus, and Thomas eventually defined himself as straight. Yet clearly others had begun defining something else about Suwai: he was a person they trusted, a good listener, and a leader.

Despite his confident demeanor, Suwai now admits that "before camp, I was afraid of expressing myself fully. Part of me thought I should be ashamed of my sexuality." Speaking up at camp helped him to gain confidence, especially in front of a big group of people, and to share himself openly and freely. But it's not just about himself and his own growth, he believes; Suwai has come to realize that his confidence positively affects others. "Only when I share myself with others does it give them the opportunity to share themselves openly and freely with others, too," he states.

Before camp, Suwai had already sorted out the big issues surrounding his sexual orientation. During the first few weeks of that school year, Suwai had done some reading and research to educate himself on the history and politics of gender identification. Then he had decided to approach his family, beginning with his mother.

"You'll go to hell!" his mother upbraided him. "How can you do this to me? I should kick you out of the house! Cut off your college fund!" Suwai's close friends were much more accepting, but he had to survive a lot of pain as the price for his honesty.

Regardless of the impact of the race and sexuality discussion, another activity was actually the most powerful one for Suwai. Interestingly, he found that the privilege activity on Thursday surprised him most with its impact.

Delegates formed one long, shoulder-to-shoulder line outside under the redwoods. Richard directed them to take a step forward or a step back in response to the statements he read. "This is a silent activity," he added. "Step forward or back based on your understanding of the question, without talking to your neighbors." Some campers stole sidelong glances at the person next to them, then grasped hands as Richard instructed.

"Take a step forward if your house had at least fifty books in it," he instructed. Students also stepped forward if their parents encouraged them to attend college, if their family owned its own home, if they saw people who looked like them on TV or in their textbooks, or if their parents told them they could be anything they wanted to be. These were a sample of the privileges many people were born with or were granted by the hard work, generosity, and grace of their parents or caregivers.

On the other hand, interspersed among these positive statements were more sobering ones. "Take one step back," Richard paused to make eye contact with the group, "if one or both of your parents never finished college. Take one step back if one of your parents was ever laid off from a job," or "If your family ever went hungry because there wasn't enough money for food." Richard continued, "Take one step back if your ancestors came to this country against their will or if your family came to America to escape poverty or political persecution." As campers stepped forward or back, they eventually lost contact with their neighbors, dropping their hands, severing the connection.

At the end of this activity, participants were ranged around the blacktop with a startling disparateness. Some, often the lighter skinned, had moved far enough forward as to be up against the fence under the eaves of the main hall. Others, mostly the darkest skinned, were so far back as to be in the redwood chapel area near the swings. This was where Suwai found himself. His family had fled Burma due to poverty and persecution. Suwai recalls eating only rice and drinking only water for days on end because there was nothing else. Their house had burned down twice, and though his grandfather had been wealthy, the new so-called government had seized everything. A number of Richard's statements resonated with Suwai, and from his stand at the back of the group, he gained a visual representation of all the trying things he had been through. And it wasn't just questions regarding poverty or family opportunity that caused Suwai to step backwards. "Take a step back if you were ever teased due to your race, gender, ethnicity, or sexual orientation," Richard directed. Statements like that caused Suwai to step back farther and farther.

"The privilege activity really helped me to realize how far I'd come to be where I am right now," Suwai reflects. "All the negative things I've been through made me into the positive person I am today." So many things had conspired to hold him back, yet Suwai completed the activity feeling proud of all he had overcome. The activity can demonstrate what privileges and hardships life has handed people but not what they've done with it. For Suwai, it also helped him realize that he was surrounded by support and resources that could help him thrive.

Suwai left camp with an even stronger sense of self. He had learned to bridge the barrier between himself and others who he had previously thought "were less or more than me," as he put it. He talked more with people who were different from him and especially made an effort to befriend others.

After camp, Suwai's self-esteem continued to grow. Because he now felt more accepted for his sexual orientation, he began to dress more feminine, sometimes wearing eye shadow to school.

Back on campus, one boy taunted, "Hey, are you a girl or a guy?" as he used his belt to poke Suwai in the rear.

Suwai turned on the kid, saying calmly, "You know that's harassment, and I could report you for it. Stop treating me that way." Suwai's words and confidence disarmed his harasser.

Yet it wasn't all a smooth path after that. These

new insights started to fade after about six months. Suwai was sucked back into the cliques and norms surrounding him in his senior year of high school. Nevertheless, in college and in the community, he was able to attend other seminars or read books on his own that refreshed his heightened consciousness. Camp had provided a foundation, but "it's important to keep things going," Suwai says. "You have to practice it to remember it. There needs to be a way for people to hold the knowledge in place and keep it alive."

His growth continued. Through a friend's dad, Suwai learned about the Landmark Education training, which claims to increase the quality of people's relationships, their personal success, and their enjoyment of life. "After attending that seminar, my life got turned upside down for the better," recounts Suwai. He subsequently increased his confidence, which in turn increased his ability to communicate honestly with others. This time, when Suwai approached a family member—his dad—about his sexual orientation, his dad replied, "No matter what you are, you'll always be my son, and I'll love you." Suwai was beginning to manifest more and more good things in his life. As the privilege activity had shown him, he could achieve what he wanted by accessing many resources as well as using his capabilities.

"I learned to see what was stopping me from being what I wanted to be," Suwai explains. He has gone on to pursue multiple artistic endeavors, including showing his photos and creating a demo CD of his music. And he has continued to be a role model for others.

"After camp, I was totally inspired to work with people and to educate others," he states. He has been an art counselor at the San Jose Museum of Art and has also worked with the YMCA as part of an elementary school series of art workshops.

Suwai would like to be trained to lead camp himself. He's already returned as an adult counselor multiple times. He says about camp, "No matter how old or young you are, there's a value for you if you give it a shot. It's one of life's most valuable privileges to be a part of it."

Pathway to Peace

"Okay, we finished the 'getting to know you' activity, so you know each other's names," Bianca stated to the circle of teens. "Now let's take some time to debrief last night's racism activity." Delegates were flopped around the lounge on an assortment of furniture, from a frumpy, flowered couch to a faded blue cushion on the floor to an overstuffed orange chair.

"Oh man," burst out Roberto, "that was pretty intense." He rubbed his hands over his shorn head and then looked at the others.

"What were you feeling or thinking when you saw those words?" pressed Bianca, urging Roberto to elaborate. As she leaned forward, her many long braids swung loose, framing her face, though she crackled with focused intensity. Bianca was like a shot of espresso: small, dark brown, and energizing.

"When I saw all those words on the poster like 'wetback' and 'dirty Mexican,' I was really pissed. I wanted to know who said that," Roberto said.

Bianca's co-facilitator Mitch spoke up, hoping to mollify Roberto's anger. "Remember, the words were stereotypes or slurs people had heard about that group before. It didn't mean that they believed those things."

Bianca wanted to help Roberto get to the core of his feelings, to understand the experience fully, not just settle for his initial reaction. She continued, "So where do you think those stereotypes come from?" Even at age nineteen, Bianca was the most petite person in the group, though her mighty yet even-tempered presence more than made up for it.

"People probably say those things because they're stupid," suggested Roberto. "It's ignorance, man. They don't know me."

Veronica joined the conversation and added, "Yeah, maybe they've never known a Mexican person before. They just saw something on TV and thought that was true about every Mexican." She rubbed her hands down her jeans.

"Or maybe they just want to hurt people," Angela, a honey-skinned Filipina, spoke up. "You know, people say mean things, but they're really just trying to feel better about themselves."

Alonso, a Latino, spoke up, "Man, if my dad heard someone call him a beaner or a wetback, he'd be so mad!"

The lively exchange continued as each delegate had the opportunity to talk. The counselors gently prodded the delegates to work through what they had thought and felt during the previous night's activity before they moved onto questions about self-identity.

"How do we develop prejudices?" Bianca queried, "and how can we accept our prejudices and work on changing them?" Counselors are given a set of discussion group themes to follow, though of course a skilled group facilitator knows when to spend more time on a topic or when to let a participant pass and respond later.

"People got to see what words others use against them and why people call them these things," Bianca says later as she reconsiders the activity. The racism discussion helps campers see how hurtful the words really are so people will stop using them. Due to her multiple experiences as a camp counselor, Bianca has also discovered people's motivations. "They're not just saying racist remarks because it's hatred for that group but because they hear it in the media, from their families, from the people they've been around," she points out. "It's not necessarily what they feel," she continues, "but they've heard it and think it's okay to say it." Despite her kinetic energy, Bianca radiates a calm core, like a thrumming plane on the runway waiting to take off.

As Bianca reflects on the racism discussion, she recalls Richard the camp director's words. "I remember when I was a kid and people said those words: dirty Mexican." He spit them out with a hiss, the pain of that term still pricking him. "My mother always made sure that our clothes were spotless when we left the house. She scrubbed me until my skin was red," he added, "because she wanted to prove that we weren't dirty Mexicans." Others in the room nodded at Richard's recollections, an experience many of them had had as well.

"Richard is trying to put kids in touch with reality," Bianca explains, her hands gesturing outwards, "to get them to be not so caught up in what the media talks about or what their parents say, but to look outside the box." She adds, "He's willing to fly back and forth from Arizona every week just to be at camp. Richard has dedicated his life to helping kids. It takes time away from his family, but he's into making life a better place."

Though Bianca doesn't aspire to be a camp director, she hopes her role as a counselor will help her in her future profession. She wants to start as a nurse but branch out in various directions: to be a midwife, to do forensic nursing, to be a traveling nurse, to become a doctor and perform surgeries. "It will take me a long time because I want to do so much," she admits with a grin.

"I'll have to have empathy, compassion, for my patients," she explains. "People who have critical illnesses or maybe are in mental hospitals, they're trying to transform, to keep their minds intact along with their bodies.

"It's just like at camp. You have to have compassion for people who have gone through stuff, like rape or abuse. They need understanding." She forges ahead with her ideas. "They may not have told you the whole story, but you know that there's something going on." That's why Bianca wants to work on her listening skills: not only to help students as their counselor, but also to prepare for her future as a medical care provider.

On Friday, the small discussion groups met to debrief gender empowerment night. That activity often brings up delegates' experiences with harassment, abuse, rape, and other forms of violence, so it's imperative that students debrief extensively. Group members walked past the redwood grove and up the poorly paved path to the lounge where they usually met. Light shone down through the skylight of the tiny room to warm it, though the first person in still cranked on the heater against the pale March sun.

Delegates settled into their favorite soft spots. "What made you angry or sad during the activity?" Bianca queried, repeating questions that Richard had asked the night before. She looked at the delegates, encouraging them to share their feelings.

"I was really mad to see how badly the girls have been treated," said Alonso. "These are all nice girls. They don't deserve that."

"I didn't realize how many girls have been through stuff like that," said Veronica. "So many of them stood up to say they've been abused or called names."

"So what did you learn from the activity?" continued Bianca.

"That a lot of people have been hurt," answered Veronica.

"Yeah," spoke up Roberto, "I never knew that girls got hurt when I said things like that to them."

"Things like what?" prodded Bianca.

"Like calling them a ho," answered Roberto. "I ain't gonna say that no more."

"Did you see how many girls stood up for that question, the one about being called bitch or ho?" asked Mitch.

"Yeah," answered Roberto, "like almost all the girls. That's not right, man. I saw my homegirl stand up, and I was really mad that someone had talked to her like that."

As she took in what her group members were sharing, Bianca realized that, like them, she was not alone in her experiences; they all seemed to be on similar journeys. "Some of what they told me was going on in my household, too," she says later. "But it's okay to talk to someone about it. There are people who are here for you," she adds emphatically, her volume rising. Some students may not have people in their families whom they can turn to, and instead camp offers them this kind of connection and communication for the first time.

About herself, Bianca says, "Camp helped me work through my issues. I saw there's another world out there of people trying to help others." Of course, Bianca's now one of those people. "Everyone has issues, and it's okay to share them with each other. If we have an open mind, trust others, then we can get further in life together."

Bianca had followed the exchange in her group intently but had to smile inwardly. She loved it when the delegates got into the conversation, sharing their insights and feelings. As a counselor, her goal was to learn to listen more and better, to urge the delegates to speak up. "That's the hardest thing for me," she says. "I like to talk, but I'm learning to be observant, to listen, to process." She smiles widely as she talks about her experience facilitating a small discussion group. "If you can listen to people, then you'll be able to understand their character, to understand what they're going through without assuming." Bianca's put a lot of thought into this and continues, her gaze direct. "If you talk too much, then it puts your relationship with that person on hold. You don't really get to know them."

Even though she was a student at our high school and had heard a lot about camp, Bianca first attended camp as an adult counselor, once she was already a San Jose State University freshman. "If I had gone to camp in high school," she explains, "I wouldn't have taken it seriously. I was in a state of mind full of anger, and I would've taken someone else's spot, someone who could have been transformed." She had been dealing with issues at home, where she was living with her grandparents and didn't see her father much. She was not at peace with herself or the world. She also experienced strife with other kids in the Black Student Union, where she was president her junior year.

Bianca looks African American though her heritage includes Choctaw, Blackfoot, Creole, and white kin. In high school, besides involvement with the Black Student Union and the predominantly black step team Dynasty, most of her friends were Mexican. "There was a lot of drama in high school," she says, crinkling up her nose, "and also issues in my past that I had to work through. As I got older, I was ready to face reality, to not use my issues as an excuse." Bianca felt like it was time to learn more about others and to give to her community by being a camp counselor. She volunteered to be a counselor when her alma mater attended camp. "When I first got to camp, I wanted to know who would be there, if I'd know anybody," she says. But even more importantly, Bianca wondered, "I wanted to know if I'd be a good role model and do the activities properly so the students would get the most out of it."

By the last day of camp, the small discussion groups have usually grown incredibly close. Though camp is only three and a half days, it's an intense odyssey of growth. "You're like my family," the usually taciturn Alonso declared. "I've told you all things that I haven't told nobody else."

They sat lounging on the conglomeration of chairs and couches again, this time with Angela's head on Roberto's shoulder and Veronica playing with Miranda's shoelaces. The campers talked easily, like a water tap left open, their trust in each other strong.

"How can you deal with people when they say racist things?" asked Bianca. "After we go home from camp, what will you do differently? Can you take what you learned here and use it?" She looked at each delegate in turn.

"I'll just walk away if I hear racist stuff," offered Veronica.

Angela had a suggestion, too. "I'll tell people not to talk that way in front of me, that it makes me uncomfortable."

Bianca got the group to continue brainstorming, considering different scenarios: in a classroom, around their friends, with their families. "How can you help your family in understanding your experience at camp?" she asked, to move them into a new direction.

"I'll just give them a hug!" declared Roberto, holding out the "hug" necklace that was around his neck. Students had received these traditional camp gifts just before lunchtime. The hug was a little wooden clothespin person with arms made of beads representing the colors of the five major races; as the string encircled Roberto's neck, the clothespin person's "arms" hugged him. Everyone laughed and grinned at Roberto's comment before resuming the discussion. The ideas kept coming, each delegate adding a new perspective.

Bianca was proud of her group's ability to share so much, even the painful situations they'd been through. "If you don't have those hardships, how will you know how to deal with things when they come up? How will you gain wisdom?" she wonders. "Those trials in life make you stronger."

A goal of camp is to build students' capacities to communicate with others, and we also help them find resources they can access after camp. "Students don't always have a lot of people who are there for them," Bianca finds, but camp helps them so they can locate others who really are there to turn to.

"The hardships that we endure are our pathway to peace," Bianca states. She tries to live by this motto. "It's easy to say certain things," she says, "but if you can't learn to live by them, then are you really working on yourself?

"This is a test," she finishes. One she'll pass.

It's Like Walking

The young women puttered around the cabin, knowing "lights out" was in twenty minutes. Alice combed out her hair, Alex dug through her duffel bag, Hien brushed her teeth, and Nina didn't stop yakking, as usual. The wooden bed frames stuck out from the walls, each draped in a sleeping bag, pillows, and clothes, plus a few teddy bears waiting to cuddle. Angelina shuffled by in pajamas while Nina engaged Alice in further debate over the gender empowerment activity they had participated in that night. However, their Counselor-in-Training, Preet, was the only one not busy getting ready for bed. Her adult helper, who was paid to help Preet with basic hygiene chores like maneuvering out of her wheelchair to use the bathroom, had disappeared. For some reason we never discovered, the helper had taken off on the second night of camp, and Preet was left to fend for herself.

Lindsay, the teacher staying in the cabin with the girls, was the first to notice. "Hey, Preet, what's going on? Where's your helper?" she asked.

"I don't know," Preet replied, drawing out the last word. "The last time I saw her was at dinner." She fiddled with the joystick of her electric wheelchair. Her long, black hair was pulled into a ponytail, making her eyes look even bigger against her dark skin.

While one of the girls was dispatched to alert the camp organizers of the aide's disappearance, others immediately rose to the occasion. "Can we help out?" Hien asked.

"Uh, well," Preet began haltingly, "I need to take off my shoes. You can do that, I guess," she said. Hien started untying the shoelaces of Preet's blue sneakers.

Others came over to see what they could do, like finding Preet's pajamas and toothbrush in her bag. "Do you need help brushing your teeth?" Alex asked.

"No, uh, I can do that myself," Preet replied, a bit embarrassed by the fuss.

Lindsay, a young teacher still in her twenties, matter-of-factly assisted Preet to get into her pajamas and guided the other girls to help as needed. Once those needs were taken care of, however, the girls started in with their questions.

"Can you feel your thighs?" Alice asked.

"Yeah," Preet answered, "I can feel everywhere. I'm not paralyzed."

Sheryl spoke up, "Why do you lean to one side?"

Preet explained, "My muscles can't hold up my spine, so I have scoliosis."

"How long have you been in your chair?" queried Alex, hesitantly.

"Well, since I was a little kid," Preet replied. She explained that the muscular atrophy, a form of muscular dystrophy, had set in when she was only eighteen months old, so she had been like this as long as she could remember.

Nina brashly asked, "Can you have sex?"

"Uh, I don't know!" Preet responded, bewildered. "I guess so. I'm eighteen. How can I answer that? Why wouldn't I be able to?"

Despite being taken aback, Preet really didn't mind the barrage of questions. "Usually, people are very wary about asking," Preet explains later. "If you want to know something, just ask. I won't be offended." Somehow that night the walls separating Preet from her peers came down, and they used the opportunity to ask all the things they always wondered about.

Preet, her cabin mates, and the camp organizers conferred, and after a phone call to Preet's parents, they decided that Preet wouldn't need another helper brought up to camp because everyone would pitch in to help her as needed. Cabin leader Lindsay had never helped someone with these tasks before and worried that Preet would be uncomfortable, but they just went about the business like it was normal, and then it became so.

"Using the chair is just something I do. It's like walking," Preet explains.

"People automatically assume that a woman in a chair feels sorry for herself. They feel bad for me," she says. "But I'm not that person. This is the card I've been dealt. This is how I live. I'm not negative about it at all." She pauses for a moment, considering. "Being in a chair sucks sometimes, and I'm allowed to have those moments," she continues, her voice rising, "but I'm not throwing myself a pity party. People are sorry for me when they find out my condition. My response is, 'Why? I'm not.'"

There's irony in Preet's statements. She's someone who has never walked, yet her life in her chair feels as natural to her as walking is for others. Then there's the irony that this extraordinary situation—being abandoned by the caregiver and being helped by veritable strangers—was not the most important part of Preet's camp experience, which came later during the disability exercise.

Preet had had an adult helper throughout junior high school, which created a distance most of her classmates weren't able to bridge. She went to a junior high away from her elementary school friends but then chose a high school farther from home because she could reconnect with those friends she had missed. Those couple years in junior high were trying, though, with only a few friends to hang out with. "Truthfully, I had a hard time getting to know people, and I was very shy in high school," Preet explains. "I thought going to camp would help me talk to people I didn't normally talk to."

Like the body builder kid. "What's he doing at camp?" Brian asked Eddie, pointing out the white kid with the short hair and defined biceps. "Isn't he one of the jocks?"

"Yeah, he's on the football team," replied Eddie, "and I think he's a wrestler, too. His name's Jared." As usual, as campers arrived at camp, they scoped out the faces around them to see who else was there.

"I never saw most of these kids before," Brian

added. "Do they really go to our school?"

Preet had seen Jared on campus and in a class they both shared as seniors. What she didn't know was that his muscular body, athletic build, and confident stance hid a past that contained drug addicted parents, binge eating, and low self-esteem. Or that his jock persona was more apparent to others than his superior test scores and passion for knowledge.

"It was cool to get to know who he was," Preet says in retrospect. "After camp, I had an easier time going up and talking to him."

Like Jared, Preet was judged. "My chair is the main thing people look at," Preet reflects. "That's just what people do in high school. They see me as the chair person." She rolls her brown eyes a bit, though there's no bitterness in her tone.

Fortunately, camp gave others the chance to see the person in the chair, the Preet who was intelligent, talkative, ambitious, and nonjudgmental. "Camp definitely made me more outgoing," Preet says, "to break out of my shell. I realized that it was okay to make fun of myself and not be so constricted by the rules of society. I use the word 'gimp' for myself, like calling it the 'gimp ramp' instead of the wheelchair ramp. That surprises people."

For Jared, working out was like breathing; for Preet, using her chair was like walking. But could others learn to imagine what it's like to live in their skins? The disability exercise gave delegates the chance to glimpse these lives.

"Cool," thought Preet as the exercise was explained. "I know what disabilities are about. I can relate to this."

Delegates lined up to enter the main hall, and each pulled a slip of paper from a box, like a judge handing out life sentences. "You're blind now," a counselor explained as she wrapped a bright blue cloth over a delegate's eyes.

"You have no arms," explained another, taping someone's arms to his sides.

Preet's first year as a delegate, she had one arm taped down. "Hey, this isn't so bad," she chirped. "I've still got the arm I drive with. I'm used to using that one hand." She tooled around the tables to find a spot to sit and then managed to load refried beans, cheese, and salsa onto a tortilla for lunch.

But the next year, when she returned to camp as a CIT, fate dealt her a harder blow: she was blind. "How can I drive my chair?" she wailed. "I can't see!"

Tall Stephan, his dreadlocks bouncing, came to Preet's aid. He held onto the back of her chair while Preet worked the joystick. "Okay, go forty-five degrees to the left," he directed. "Now straighten out and then go ninety degrees right." Preet ran into a table.

"Okay, really, I'm blind driving a chair, and you're trying to give a math lesson now?!" she wailed at him. "This is hard enough. Don't make it any harder."

"Okay, okay," Stephan soothed, undaunted. "Let's try this again. Go left . . . left . . . a little more left. Stop." They worked out a plan that got Preet to the food and saved the other delegates from run-over toes or bumped knees.

"I've never not been able to see," Preet said to Stephan, a revelation in sudden understanding. She had never been able to walk, so why would she miss that? But sight was different.

After delegates had tried to feed themselves—and each other—despite their given disabilities, Richard called an end to the activity so everyone could finish eating. He then took the microphone from table to table. "How did you feel during this activity? What did you learn?" he asked.

Delegates shared their responses. "I felt totally helpless. I couldn't do all the things I was used to doing," said one.

Another shared, "I was trying to help the others at my table. I had one hand, so I could get the food for them." Richard moved around, eliciting various perspectives. He saved Preet for last.

"Now, you've had your disability all your life, is that right?" he queried her, the mike held to her face.

"Uh, yeah," she responded, uncomfortable being in the spotlight.

"How was this activity for you?" Richard prompted.

"Well, it was hard because I kept bumping into people," she replied, stating the obvious.

In retrospect, Preet explains, "I was shy and didn't like talking in front of people. I felt a little put on the spot. I was the 'disabled person,'" she says, making quotation marks with her fingers. "It's like asking an Asian person to give the Asian perspective." She couldn't speak for everyone else who has a disability, especially the wide variety that physical disabilities can come in. Preet felt that she could give the same kind of responses the other delegates had given: that being blind or having only one hand was challenging. But her chair had been part of her life forever. "I thought I had to say something extraordinary," she reflects, "but this is normal for me."

Still, it was an important activity for Preet. She says, smiling, "I did like the activity because it was the one I could relate to, and now everyone else could relate to me. People can finally feel the things I go through on a day-to-day basis," she reflects. Most people would label Preet as disabled, yet it was during the disability exercise that she felt what that word really implied. During her lifetime, she had learned to do nearly everything she needed to do and didn't view herself as disabled—at least not until her sight, an ability she took for granted— was taken away.

Preet gained so much from her experiences at camp: the ease of talking to others, a better ability to make friends, a chance to meet others who valued diversity and didn't judge by appearances. She explains, "Just because you think something of someone, you should still get to know them, before you make an actual judgment of them."

She also learned to speak up. "Once I went to camp," she explains, "if someone would say something stupid or racist, I would confront them on it and say, 'That was wrong.'" When she tried this with her Indian family, challenging her dad on his jokes or her brother for using the word "gay," at first she was met with some surprise. "I'd say, 'Dad, why? Why would you say that? You know it's wrong.'" They got used to her comments and later teased her about it, knowing it would bug her, but as a close family, her views were respected. Her confrontations changed the family. Preet also moved closer to a career path in marketing and public relations, the major she'll finish next year at San Jose State University—another irony, considering how shy she used to be.

But it's not just about what Preet learned. Others had the chance to learn from her, lessons like these: not everyone is disabled by a disability; not every disabled person needs or wants the same kind of help; not everyone is defined by the body she's in; not everyone knows how far forty-five degrees is.

"You see someone and think this is what they're about," Preet adds. "You can have your first impression, but don't necessarily make that the way you think about them." Like walking, we learn these lessons at different times, when we're ready to, and with baby steps. But eventually walking becomes natural.

Five to Nine

The clock read five to nine a.m.

The kids were already coming together, unifying, breaking their segregation. Bleached-blond Tammy led the insurrection.

"Take off those tags, everyone!" she called to others. "Throw them on the floor." Tammy's strident voice rose over the crowd. She led the rebellion, and at five to nine she threw her yellow patch in the middle of the floor, starting a chain reaction amongst the others. The dusty, white linoleum flashed with the brown squares for Latinos, black for African Americans, pink for gays and lesbians, white, blue, and yellow, now all piled together like confetti.

"I'm not going to go along with this any more," Tammy stated as she pulled people together to form one large mass. Her two yellow pigtails bobbed constantly at the edge of the group as she drew in one person after another. Delegates had been told to follow simple rules: they had to stay with their group at all times, and they weren't allowed to make eye contact with others outside their group, communicate, or fraternize with them. Sassy, forceful, not afraid to speak her mind, Tammy defied those rules and ended the activity five minutes before even the leaders had anticipated its termination.

Tammy was a catalyst for change. And she was only a sophomore.

Many others were right alongside her, hugging their friends, tearing off their hated construction paper squares, moving plastic chairs out of the way to make room for their growing group. The air was electric with a buzz of liberty, their enforced segregation dissolving as friends came back together to offer each other comfort and support. Marissa shed tears, as usual, with her arms around Duc, while Kenny clowned again after his unnatural silence. The room once again blossomed with laughter, which had been so conspicuously absent during the last forty-five minutes of this activity. Delegates made sure to pull in the few "isolates," students who had represented the loners in society and who had been told to stay away from everyone, look pitiable, and not make eye contact. Even when these isolates had tried to remain in their roles and stay away from the growing mass of buoyant students, Tammy and her cohorts made sure to bring them into the fold, looking each one in the eye, including them in the group.

There was some irony for Tammy as well. She had been wearing the Star of David as a member of the Jewish group, a part of her heritage that she hadn't explored much before. "I had never really faced racism," she says, "and I hadn't dealt with being Jewish. Suddenly I was in this role where I had to present on my Jewish heritage during cultural pride night and then wear the star and deal with segregation."

For the duration of the segregation activity, counselors had been instructed to enforce the rules as much as possible while remaining a "leader/non-leader"—in other words, let the delegates work through their own responses as much as possible with little instruction. In fact, Richard told counselors to keep the activity going until nine o'clock, and after that, if delegates complained about how awful the segregation was, counselors could ask them, "What do you want to do about it?"

Well, Tammy didn't even give us that much time, ending the activity early. I was inordinately proud of this firecracker who had seen through the injustice of segregation and didn't accept the norms that supported it—and also didn't wait to do something about it. Some delegates went along with the activity because they trusted the counselors and would follow their instructions; others responded to the racism that was directed at them and then reacted to it. "You can leave your dirty dishes at your tables," Richard had told everyone. "The Mexicans will clean up after you because they're good at it," he said, his voice deepening. Many of the Latinos took on the task with pride to do the job well, scrubbing tables and taking away people's plates and cups (sometimes before they were quite done with them!).

Tammy's reaction sprang from her past trials. During the gender empowerment activity two days earlier, we had learned that Tammy had been the victim of an attempted rape during her freshman year. That trauma had whittled her self-respect into a hard little bone, but her ability to look that experience in the face, as well as good counseling and parenting, had helped her to see that she could survive anything. She declares now, "I was not going to be limited by the roles others placed upon me."

Then Friday's privilege activity had shown Tammy another of her assets: her loving and supportive family. While some people took steps forward in the line to represent the positive things life had given them, Tammy found herself moving to the back of the group due to her family's poverty, one of the few white faces back by the redwood grove. But during the debriefing she was able to see the jewel in her difficult life experience. "I was pushed to excel," Tammy explains, "so I learned that money was less important compared to family support. I came from a family that had little, but look what I've been able to accomplish anyway," she says, spreading her arms as if to encompass all the gifts that surround her.

On that Saturday morning, however, her vehemence was mostly directed at Richard, the camp director, who played the role of oppressor and authoritarian during the segregation activity. He enforced the rules and even instigated trouble. For example, he took away the Asian group's deck of cards and slammed the door in the face of the African American group, who were last to enter the hall. "You people are always last," he asserted as we all snuck covert glances when they stopped in place like they'd been slapped. Richard instructed the white students to get some food; "You get to eat first," he pointed out. He was highlighting the role our society maintains for each group.

After having gone through the activity, Tammy says of Richard, "He's the guy you love to hate," though she also admits, "He asked all the right questions that you didn't want to answer, but you knew you should." It was a pretty intense activity but also a huge learning experience, one participants never forget.

Saturday morning's segregation activity was a final test of sorts, to see what delegates had learned, but even more so it was a pre-test to predict how they might fare back in general society. Would they fall prey to the pressure to conform to society's norms, such as segregation? Would they collapse back into the familiar patterns they had before coming to camp? Or would they take a stand against divisive norms and ridiculous unwritten rules and instead unify people?

After the students ended the segregation and came back together as a group, they spent a couple hours debriefing the entire exercise, with special attention on the experiences of people in different roles. Richard began by asking, "Why did we do this?"

Many hands went up. Delegates responded that they needed to see how they would react back in the "real world" where segregation and prejudice were everyday facts in their schools. Brian explained, "On every campus, students clump together in groups most often based on race, and we hear racist remarks daily."

"This is also a history lesson," Tammy added. "This is how people were really treated, like the signs you put up in the bathrooms for 'whites only' and 'colored only,'" she pointed out to Richard. Students had varied reactions to these signs, such as the biracial students' confusion about which toilet to use or one student of color who threw the sign in the toilet and urinated on it.

"You wanted us to experience these feelings ourselves," added one camper, "not just talk about them."

The forced segregation activity gives delegates that visceral experience of segregation and is modeled after what has become known as the "blue-eyed/brown-eyed experiment." Third grade teacher Jane Elliot designed a lesson where she segregated students by eye color, and she first told the blue- and green-eyed children that they were superior to the brown-eyed ones. Children with blue and green eyes received more praise, more recess time, and other privileges. The children quickly got caught up in their roles, with blue-eyed kids harassing and bullying a brown-eyed classmate. When she had students switch roles, students quickly took up their new roles, calling each other names and even resorting to violence. At camp, Richard put people into roles based on race, religion, or sexual orientation, himself playing the role of harasser in a controlled way that still got the point across.

During the debriefing, Richard also wanted to know, "Is it better that we did this activity on the last day, or should we have done it right when you got off the bus?" Though there were some dissenters, most students agreed that it made a better test of their true learning for them to do this activity at the end, after they had bonded with their new friends. When they stepped off the bus, most students stayed attached to their friends, but at the end of the segregation activity, the jocks were hugging the gay kids, the Asians were reaching out to the blacks, everyone was forming one unified group.

"I was so sad when I couldn't talk to my friends," responded Amanda.

Marissa looked over at Mary and said, "I saw my friend crying, and I couldn't do anything about it."

Tammy had been outraged because it reminded her of what she saw in society around her. "People always separate themselves from each other based on nothing more than assumptions and ignorance," she asserts. But for Tammy, anger always spurred her to action.

Though anger may move her, Tammy's desire to improve things is the stronger imperative. Camp made her want to help others more, to take a negative and turn it into a positive. "I want to be a tool to help people grow," Tammy tells others. "Life goes on, and it gets better as it goes. You make your own life and happiness," she philosophizes. After camp, she was on this new path with a passion.

When Tammy had arrived at camp on Wednesday afternoon, her first thought had been, "Oh crap, what did I get myself into?" But by Saturday morning, when faced with segregation that her gut told her was wrong, she was all action: organizing, cajoling, leading. It was the emotional content of camp that pulled her forward to places she hadn't explored before. "I've always been a leader," Tammy admits, "but camp helped me grow in my leadership skills."

Tammy took her leadership skills and had somewhere to direct them. She began by becoming active in the diversity club back on campus, and she now returns to camp as a counselor a couple times a year and has done so for half a dozen years. In fact, she's one in a family dynasty of sorts; both parents, her brother, and two cousins have all been to camp either as delegates, counselors, or both. Tammy's bleached-blond hair has grown out brown, but she still finds physical expression in her collection of tattoos, from a row of stars below one ear to the dragon on her shoulder. Though she may seem like a scrapper that you want on your side in a fight, she's also the most gentle soul who has helped raise over eighty foster children in her parents' home.

While others may conform to the rules to remain safe or wait for a leader to appear, Tammy will be the one out there in front, five minutes ahead of the rest.

We Need You

"I don't know if I can make it to camp, Ms. Meyers," Nima told his English teacher a few days after his initial show of interest. "I don't want to miss my classes." The three of us stood outside after class, Nima ducking his head in apology with his hands in the pockets of his baggy jeans.

"But Nima, we need you," Lindsay Meyers responded, shading her eyes against the bright sun. "We don't have any Muslim or Middle Eastern students attending camp."

I was surprised to hear her say this to him, thinking that this comment could put undue pressure on a fifteen-year-old, or put him on the spot to speak for an entire religion or a geographic region. Instead, it seemed to be the note that struck a chord in Nima, propelling him toward attending camp. He cocked his head at an angle. "I'll think about it," he said.

It was a couple years after September 11, 2001, and negative stereotypes about Middle Easterners and Muslims seemed to be solidifying in the nation's mind. As we recruited for camp, we felt an added pressure to find students representing this region and religion. As usual, camp is a place where delegates meet people from different backgrounds and get to know them as individuals, and we hoped that camp could be a forum where students could discover that people with Middle Eastern heritage weren't all terrorists or religious extremists.

So we really needed Nima.

But as it turned out, Nima needed camp.

"I used to be into my Persian roots during my freshman year," Nima told me, "but I didn't know enough about my culture to be close to it. My family celebrated the holidays, and we sometimes speak Farsi at home, but that's about it." Even so, to look at this sophomore in his oversized sweatshirt and Van's skater shoes, you might not discern his ethnicity at all. Nima is built slight but lean as both a football player and track athlete. He wears his curly, dark brown hair very short, and I can only ever remember him with his goatee, even as a sophomore. At a previous camp, I had known another Middle Eastern student who dressed like the Mexican gangster kids, wearing his black Ben Davis sagging pants and oversized white t-shirts, trying to blend in with that race rather than claim his own. Was Nima doing something similar? I didn't yet know him well enough to understand how he viewed his Persian heritage. Was he simply a fashion-conscious teen or someone trying to blend in so well as to erase his identity?

Once at camp, Nima took our words seriously; if he was needed, then he would rise to the occasion and speak up. He emitted the electric idealism of youth but at this point lacked direction. "I wasn't nervous arriving at camp," he remembers. "I just wanted to hurry up and get things going. I wanted the program to begin, to start the process, minus the intro stuff," he says, leaning forward to emphasize his point.

Things got hopping immediately, during our group discussion on racism the first night. After volunteers had recorded the list of stereotypes about Middle Easterners, Nima felt compelled to speak. His lip curled, and he groaned when he saw the common stereotypes scrawled on butcher paper: towel head, camel jockey, suicide bomber. One person can't dispel an entire stereotype, but Nima enacted the best approximation I had yet seen. With a wave of his hand, he dismissed the ignorance behind the remarks. Then he pulled up his t-shirt. "See, no bombs here," he said sarcastically. Maybe not without his rancor showing, yet still with fair and insightful assessments, Nima explained what life in Iran was really like, including an emphasis on family and education.

He hadn't yet educated himself about Iran's culture or politics; that knowledge would come later. Nonetheless, still incensed by the words he had seen scrawled on the posters, Nima also told the group about a student back on campus who had blurted out that he "wanted to join the army to kill those fuckers for what they did to us," referring to the misconception that Iran was responsible for the 9/11 attacks. Nima told us how he had gotten angry and answered the boy, only half kidding, "Maybe you need to get shot. Please go to war." The list of stereotypes had sparked off an anger that Nima normally contained.

Usually an evening less serious in tone, Friday

night at camp was cultural pride night. Campers had arranged chairs in a big horseshoe facing the brick fireplace, and MCs scribbled the line up onto an easel pad. Groups had had a couple meetings to follow Richard's directive: "Create a skit, game show, or presentation that shares your group's major contributions and immigration patterns to America and also addresses or dispels stereotypes about your group." Delegates colored flags on posters, rehearsed Viking invasions and cumbia dances, and dug out sarongs and spaghetti pots for such diverse groups as Italians and African Americans to Blended Americans, Jews, and gays and lesbians. Because Nima hadn't spent much time studying his culture yet, he merely presented information on oil as a resource in the Middle East, and he even coerced one of the counselors to belly dance. The fact that he had little to contribute was the unfortunate consequence of not knowing much about Iran at the time. That realization spurred Nima to further expand his knowledge about his culture. "Camp was another wake up call to learn more," he says now.

In fact, it also made him review his beliefs about racism. He acknowledges having some racist beliefs earlier, but "There are no loopholes in racism," he contends. "You can't say you love a certain kind of white person, for example, and disparage the rest. That's contradictory." Nowadays, Nima focuses on creating unity and inclusiveness.

On the last night at camp, we all sat in one large circle and passed a candle, using our moment with it to give thanks, recite a quote, or share final thoughts. I think of the candle that night as igniting a flame within Nima, a flame that would be the heat under his seat to set him in motion.

Because after that camp, Nima was on fire.

Back at school, Nima attended all club meetings. He would stand on a chair to get the room's attention. Though we already had club officers, Nima started shadowing Jeremy, the president, to learn the job. Nima became club president for the next two years and started the tradition of grooming future officers.

"Camp taught me how to be a leader, how to manage different situations, how to move people into positions to get work done," Nima explains. "It taught me how to express everything and not hide anything." Under his leadership, the club put on its first conference with workshops that furthered camp ideals and goals. The conference included a video and discussion about hate crimes and a panel discussion on gay and lesbian issues. Nima got kids to meet after school, and he even coerced me to meet with him over vacation to make plans for future events. "I learned how to take an idea and make it a reality," he says.

Camp changed Nima in the classroom, as well. "During class discussions," he recalls, "I had often feared teachers' criticism." Not any more. Now he realized that he had to take a stand, to offer his contribution, and from camp he gained the confidence to do so.

Nima returned to camp as a Counselor-in-Training and again, after graduating high school, as an adult counselor. In fact, when Nima attended camp during his freshman year of college, he experienced a small crisis of leadership. Nima probably belongs on a soapbox, where his declamatory oratorical style can motivate large crowds and call the apathetic to action. So when he took charge too often rather than allowing new delegates to step up to new-found leadership, he took it out on himself. He pulled me aside while others sang songs around the campfire one night. "I should take myself out of the program," he told me while we stood at the edge of the forest's darkness. "I'm afraid I'm doing more harm than good. I don't know when to keep my mouth shut, and I talk too much." Nima raised his eyes to the stars peeking through the canopy of redwoods.

He was experiencing the growing pains of any leader, finding his style amidst changing roles and needs. Upon further reflection, Nima realized, "I learned to facilitate and not just take over. Camp emphasizes asking questions and how to engage others. It teaches you to be a better leader."

Just like Nima's first time at camp, on the last night everyone gathered in the main hall for the candle-light ceremony. The white linoleum floor was bespattered with redwood needles and dirt, so a counselor hastily swirled the long, flat broom around to sweep away the worst of it while campers arranged seventy-something chairs in an enormous circle. This ceremony was the oldest tradition at camp, an activity that remains unchanged after fifty-plus years.

Once everyone had taken a seat, Richard explained the process. "Each of you will have a moment with this candle," he began, one knee on the floor, his gaze moving from person to person. "This is your chance to address the group. You can share a quote or poem, you can tell what camp means to you, or you can thank people." He held up an unimpressive white candle stub in a star-shaped glass. "We'll turn off the lights now and begin," he finished.

The candle passed from hand to hand, some campers setting it on the floor, and others holding it while they spoke. Each was highlighted in its glow, faces illuminated against the black backdrop. When the candle reached Nima, he read these words from Jim Wallace, "Tonight, we don't just light candles, we make a commitment . . . . There are many dark places in the world where unspeakable violence against large numbers of innocent people is being planned. Let those places be exposed to the light of day and the violence be thwarted." Nima's light was stronger than any doubts; his commitment was total. Like that small candle that could illuminate both a face and a whole room, Nima's spirit could dispel darkness wherever he found it. In growing to his complete leadership potential, Nima still needed camp. Camp, of course, still profited from his presence.

The fire inside Nima still hasn't diminished. Now at Santa Clara University, Nima has joined clubs that work for social justice and focus on cultural issues; in fact, he's spearheading a push to expand the multicultural clubs into the campus. He's studying both Farsi and Spanish and plans to spend a whole summer in Iran as well as time in Mexico. But Nima is apologetic that he hasn't already changed the world. He explains, "I'm young. I just need more education and more time."

Still No Band-Aids

"I'm glad I met you not as a teacher, but as a friend."

"I can see you possess the unique ability to spread your knowledge and love to a large number of young adults, and it makes me realize that you are one of the teachers that will never be forgotten by your students."

"You are down to earth and have a loving mystique. You are all that a good friend is, patient and understanding."

"You're everything you want a mother to be."

"You're open-minded, compassionate, and unforgettable."

These words, written carefully on notebook paper, are now always tucked into Tracy's wallet. Refolded or pulled out countless times since the first time Tracy went to camp in 1997, these pages from five camps repeat to Tracy her many good qualities as a teacher, mother, leader, and friend. These pronouncements acted as a balm against the wounds the world could inflict.

The kind words were the product of the affirmation exercise, a final activity on Saturday afternoon that left everyone glowing. Seven students and their two small discussion group leaders lounged outside hoping to soak up the freckles of sunlight that sprinkled through the redwood trees where they sat on logs or the chairs they had dragged outside from the office. Tom had the white notepad and tried to write quickly, keeping a record as each person told Tracy the great things about her. Tracy, usually running her world like a tight ship, instead sat back as a participant and let the praise wash over her. She stretched her long legs in front of her and occasionally flipped her blond hair off her neck, smiling.

"You made this group like a family. You let me care for you," Jessica wrote as she peered up at Tracy from under her brows.

Caitlyn said, "You have an aura that I can trust." These were both girls who needed a strong woman they could look up to.

But TJ needed something else. He was all honesty. "I didn't like you last year as a teacher, but being in as informal an environment as this changed how I view you as a person." He didn't smile as he said it, but that didn't faze Tracy. She could see his sincerity from his direct gaze.

Others in the discussion group added their praise. "You're easy to bond with," said Josh, while Christi told her, "I know I can go to you."

"Why thank you," Tracy replied, one hand on her round belly. This would be Tracy's last camp before leaving teaching to bear Dimitri, whom she'd stay home to rear. The moment in the speckled sunshine seemed to stretch out. Both the students who had known her for a while and the ones who had just met her at camp knew this was a moment to savor. "Well, who shall we talk about next?" asked Tracy, breaking the spell and moving on to make sure each student had a turn to be praised.

"What I like best about camp is the affirmation exercise," Tracy states in reflection, "especially when the kids are putting thought into it." Tracy brightens and sits up straighter as she recalls the many nice things students listed about her. Though Tracy is a model of strong self-esteem and solid self-confidence, her most powerful camp experience proves to be the one where people stroke her ego. People might never guess that she wanted or maybe even needed that praise, which just goes to show that all people love to be told how wonderful they are.

As much as she loved the affirmation exercise though, it was not the activity that opened Tracy's eyes to parts of society that she hadn't truly noticed before, nor was it the activity that changed her the most. Regarding race relations, Tracy recalls, "I thought I was already smart enough and knew this stuff. My own thoughts and feelings on the way the world was, well, some of those changed, even at the age of forty-plus." The privilege exercise had the most impact, shaking her out of her comfortable worldview as a middle-class, white woman. This was the activity where Richard read statements about the privileges people are born with or the curve balls life throws at some, such as job loss or eviction, and participants take steps forward or backward to symbolize the effects of these events on their lives. After taking more steps forward than back, Tracy found herself at the front of the group, standing under the eaves of the main hall. Growing up, she had had the privileges of a stable home filled with books and loving parents who had emigrated from England to America by choice, not due to war or oppression as many immigrants experience. "Take a step forward if your parents told you that you could be anything you wanted to be," Richard directed the group, and Tracy smiled as she took that step forward, recalling her loving mum.

But later during the small group debriefing, things were different. "What did you do to earn the privilege to be born white?" one member of her discussion group asked Tracy in a very matter-of-fact tone. Tracy was stunned—not offended, because she had built up enough trust and honesty in her group that they could say such things to each other. However, Tracy had never thought about her life in those terms before. While her mouth dropped open in speechlessness, a state she rarely experienced, the delegates looked at her in anticipation, sensing that she would respond thoughtfully. "I never thought of that before," she finally said, her head tilted to the side.

"I had done nothing to earn the privileges society accorded me," Tracy reports. She refers to the advantages that most middle-class, white Americans enjoy such as access to any housing or job, exemption from discrimination, freedom from suspicion, and admission to superior schools. "As a white woman, I am not followed around in a shop, store workers put my change in my hand and not on the counter, and I am not seen as a threat to many based on the color of my skin," Tracy explains. "Wherever I go, if I speak well, I am able to get almost anything I want, even talk my way out of a ticket or two," she finishes with a wry smile.

Thinking back to that discussion group, Tracy realizes, "It was a wake-up call to remind myself to not be stuck in my white world and to be more sensitive to other people's misfortune. Not everyone was born white and to these privileges." While Tracy understands the privileges that society affords her without any effort on her part, she also realizes that it works against others. For example, simply due to skin color, some people experience police harassment, job discrimination, lowered expectations, and even violence.

Tracy, who spent some years as a single mom of two boys, married a second time and decided to have another child so her husband could experience having a child of his own. When Tracy left teaching to have Dimitri, we hated to see such a strong teacher leave our profession, and we grieved over the void in the social studies department. Yet Tracy is now happy to devote herself to raising Dimitri, and she plans to return to teaching—and to camp–one day. For the moment her focus is motherhood.

Tracy's beliefs about motherhood were challenged during conversations at camp with Clarissa. One of the staff members who organizes camp from the head office, Clarissa usually comes up to camp for one day of each group's stay. An African American mom in a threatening world, she has fought many battles and spent countless fearful days raising her sons. Like Tracy, Clarissa isn't afraid to speak about difficult truths of life.

The first time Tracy and Clarissa met, they stood in the main meeting hall and talked as mothers. With her hands on her hips, Clarissa said, "I used to tell my son every day as he went out the door, 'Don't be at the wrong place at the wrong time.' A young black man is ten times more likely to be killed than a young white man, and I had to look out for my son's safety." Her volume rose, and her eyes grew rounder.

Then Clarissa looked up at the taller woman and said, "You don't have to do that because you're white." It was a simple statement of fact, not an accusation.

Once again, Tracy's mouth dropped open, stunned. But she is nothing if she's not an honest, forthright person, and she appreciated this kind of directness from others. After a moment, she found her voice. "You're right," she stated.

Later, Tracy reflected. "I wasn't offended," Tracy says. "I was enlightened. I was also a bit embarrassed that I had never had to put myself into a black person's shoes," she says. "It woke me up and reminded me that I'm not all-knowing when it comes to race relations. Clarissa's comment stuck in my mind a lot, even years later."

Clarissa's life experiences affected Tracy in other ways, as well. Tracy, a feminist herself, recognized that society had made two strikes against Clarissa from the outset, as an African American and as a woman. Both groups face greater chances of discrimination and inequality. To try to counter that, during gender empowerment night Tracy is a cheerleader for the girls. "They already have one strike against them as women," Tracy realizes as she thinks about the way our country works, with only sixteen percent of our current senators being women—and that's the highest it's ever been. Though we currently have one of the most racially diverse congresses our country has ever seen, racial minorities still only total nineteen percent, and that number drops to fourteen percent if Jewish congress members aren't included. Tracy, a wife and mother of three boys, nevertheless feels especially called to empower young women. "Girls need to work harder, work smarter, and take themselves seriously," Tracy says. "I try to help them live up to their potential." Camp is one place where she gets to do that most effectively, sharing with them statistics about women in politics or the workplace, giving career advice, and conferring one-on-one about their self-image and aspirations. She can't play doctor to all the world's ills, but she can do much to promote perseverance and optimism.

The delegates get it, and Tracy's affirmations confirm this. That's why Tracy received such statements as, "You're a great women's role model. I respect the way you bring out female gender;" "You taught us to look at things the right way;" and "You always want to know why, and you're in balance with yourself."

"My sons call me 'Gandhi behind the wheel' now because I'm overly sensitive to others and let them all pass me on the road," Tracy explains with a laugh. "I'm much more sensitive to people of color," she adds, "and to people who don't have the means to send their kids to preschool or private school, which means your child is already behind. I'm hypersensitive to people not recognizing their own prejudice.

"There are no Band-Aids for people who are black or Hispanic," Tracy points out as a literal example. "Our society is still designed with white people in mind. Still the pale-faced Band-Aid!"

Figuratively speaking, there are no Band-Aids for our society, either. There's no quick fix or panacea. But camp goes a long way towards raising awareness. It helps kids to gain confidence, improve their communication, and begin to be advocates for themselves and for each other. Each of them leaves camp with a little rectangle of praise. Carrying a wallet full of affirmations may not be a Band-Aid to make all wounds disappear, but in a hurtful or frightening world, it's often a salve.

Be the Change

"Be the change you want to see in the world."
–Mahatma Gandhi

The quiet Asian girl sat straight-backed in the desk in my classroom, eyes following the lesson attentively, occasionally fingering her long, black hair. She answered questions when called upon, asked for clarification to make sure she was getting things right, and turned in meticulous work. Shy and relatively solitary, she had a few casual friends in class but was not the type who left class giggling with a group or who received bouquets of balloons on her birthday. Helen seemed intent on living up to the "model minority" stereotype so many people hold about Asian Americans: that they succeed academically, work hard, and stay out of trouble.

I had told my freshman English class about our lunchtime meeting being held that day for the diversity club that I advised. Everyone was welcome, and we'd be going over details about camp for anyone who was interested in attending. "That might be a good way to meet people," thought Helen, who wanted to broaden her circle of friends. She started attending club meetings, but it would be two years before Helen decided it was time to go to camp.

Yet the desire to meet new people and her native curiosity for a new experience were strong enough to help Helen get past her trepidation, plus it was a rare field trip! On winding Highway 9, the kids on the bus were noisy; with wry humor, Helen thought, "High schoolers are constitutionally incapable of being quiet on a bus ride." As the big, yellow school bus pulled into the camp parking lot, Helen's stomach did a nervous dance. "How will people perceive me?" she wondered. She saw the rich diversity in races around her and suddenly realized that she had never really interacted nor lived near people besides whites and Asians.

Reflecting on these feelings later, Helen recalls, "The media showed me that there was a lot of friction between blacks, Latinos, and Asians. Also my grandpa's experiences of racism and his own prejudices against blacks and Latinos probably had an effect on me even though I thought I was the type to try to be open to everything and everybody." Tilting her head, she continues, "When I watch the news, I think of all the potential negative things people are thinking about me, about Asians," she worries. "I feel intimidated by those stereotypes."

Helen carried this baggage to camp along with her suitcase and sleeping bag. She fretted, "What are my own biases? Am I going to show these to others, maybe blurt out something dumb? How will they be looking at me?"

Helen may have been solitary when she arrived

at camp, but it didn't last long. Student counselors and staff greeted her with clapping and maniacally friendly grins, and she soon was toting her bags to her cabin to meet the girls she would share it with. Debra, a mahogany-skinned girl in a bright orange sweatshirt, bounced along, cracking wise and laughing. Helen took an immediate liking to her enormous smile and upbeat energy. "Hey girlfriend, let me help you with that bag," Debra offered genially. Cabin mates often grew quite close as eight people shared one bathroom, tossed candy to each other, or stayed awake chatting after "lights out." Cabin groups were also assigned kitchen duty, setting out or clearing plates for the whole camp, working together.

Later, Helen got to meet others at the dinner table. One who befriended her early on was Alvaro, a solidly-built but gentle Latino with a soft voice and accent. "Hi, my name's Alvaro," he offered. "I don't think I've seen you at school before."

"No, I don't think so," answered Helen. "Who do you have for math?"

Their conversation continued from there and on to other days. Maybe because he stood calmly or moved deliberately, Alvaro seemed more thoughtful than most. Helen noticed how he always looked others in the eye, not rattling on in every conversation, but sharing his thoughts with sincerity.

After dinner, campers dragged their screeching chairs into a huge circle under the blond beamed ceilings of the main hall. Before Richard could begin discussing the ground rules, someone called out, "Rainbow!" Everyone scrambled across the room to find a new seat, making sure to mix it up. "Don't sit next to someone who's the same race or gender as you!" Richard explained using the mike as people skidded into their new seats. Helen found herself next to Scott, a Native American man who wore his salt and pepper hair in thin braids. As she got to know him that night and at subsequent activities, Helen realized that he was secure in his identity and radiated a calm presence. Scott had a practice of giving people Native American names to fit their personality or actions. "Knowing him," says Helen, "did something good for my head."

The second day at camp, students formed yet another group, their small discussion group, for debriefing the activities and for having deeper discussions on issues like understanding one's self, friendships, peer leadership, and family cultures. A laid-back white kid named Robbie was in Helen's group, and while she had had plenty of interactions with Caucasians in her life, she had never met one with dreadlocks who spouted his spoken-word poems with such passion and force. Even his woolen hat with its ear flaps and dangling tassels only enhanced his cool factor. "Hey man," Robbie began, "I think I saw you at the last poetry club meeting." His slow smile spread in greeting.

The small discussion group took time to praise each other, something Helen hadn't experienced enough in her sixteen years. Her group met in an empty cabin, where they had pulled the wooden bed frames into a circle and sat on the bare mattresses. The group leaders led them through the affirmation activity, taking the time for each camper to be praised by all the others while a volunteer recorded these statements on notebook paper for the recipient to keep. "You're sweet and kind," someone said, and, "You're a good listener." Helen smiled gratefully. But best of all, one person responded, "You're brave enough to talk in discussions." Helen, brave? This gave her a new perception of herself, one she liked and wanted to cultivate.

Not a gregarious person (yet!), Helen spent much time during her first days at camp watching others, listening, taking it all in. "I was sort of self-aware of my personal prejudices and biases," she recalls, but she also saw them melting away as she slowly bonded with others: exuberant Debra, thoughtful Alvaro, earnest Robbie, steady Scott.

Helen also realized that others were going through the same things as her. She wasn't the only one feeling self-conscious or vulnerable. She wasn't the only one afraid to speak up. "I realized I wasn't alone," she reflects. This realization especially struck home during the gender empowerment activity, when first the men and then the women stood silently when they heard the statements about things their group had experienced. The men and women sat in separate groups, facing each other, silently noting the others' frowns, downcast eyes, defiant stares, hunched shoulders, tears. "Talking about things on an emotional level is really fricking hard," Helen states now. "Standing up is easier than talking about things, but it's still really powerful." This silent activity fit her comfort level, giving her a way to join in.

Indeed, her powers of reflection and perception

were her strongest ways to participate. When she saw one of her teachers stand up, admitting that he had abused a woman to keep her in her place, Helen realized how brave people are. "He was willing to stand up and say, 'This has happened to me.' The guys really got it then," she says, understanding what the stereotypes are and what people have gone through. What we see on the outside of people is not the whole story. This gave her insight into others and a desire to get to know their full stories, not just the person they showed to others. But also, the realization gave her permission to show her true self. "All the experiences and knowledge stewed around in my head for quite a while," she reflected, "and then I was ready to talk about it and not sound like an idiot."

It was as if someone had thrown open a door and extended a hand in invitation. While Helen had been journeying towards that doorstep for a few years, she now was ready to enter a new realm. Helen became a prime mover in the club on campus, helping to organize monthly potlucks, panel discussions, and guest speakers. "What do you want to do for the next potluck?" she'd ask. "It's Hispanic Heritage Month.

"I learned to talk to people I didn't know, to make conversation," she adds in reflection. "Camp gave me the confidence to just start talking with people and trying to find points of commonality, to dive in and connect with people, which of course is the most important way to destroy stereotypes, by building those connections."

Then for her senior year, Helen returned to camp

as a CIT. "I had a better idea of why I felt the way I did," she says now, "and had a better way of expressing how I felt or why I did what I did."

Helen also spent a lot of time questioning things, including her own racial identity. Her heritage is Chinese, but she was born in the U.S. and felt pulled between both cultures. Even so, she sometimes introduced herself as Asian American for political reasons, uniting with other Asians who had experienced similar stereotypes as she had. Many people have found that there can be more power in the unity of race.

After high school, Helen moved to Southern California to attend Scripps College. Once there, she discovered that at this primarily white liberal arts college, most people didn't want to discuss race. "Students of color don't want to make waves there," she noted. "They just want to get their education and go." There were still the old stereotypes, albeit more sophisticated than their high school versions. "We were seen as Asians when we were useful to others, and then we were closer to being accepted by whites," Helen found, "but when we were threatening, we were grouped with other people of color."

Helen had studied French, Mandarin, Spanish, and even Japanese and decided to major in sociolinguistics. Her studies helped her understand how one's gender, ethnicity, age, class, religion, and education affected one's use of language and thus one's status and power. Language usage can create an imbalance of power between people or groups. "These theories explained a lot about how I was treated," says Helen when she later reflected on her choice of major. "Not overt racism, but stereotyping, whitewashing, subversion of political correctness." With a raised shoulder, she adds, "It was hard because in high school and early college, I would encounter situations that made me so angry, but I couldn't articulate properly why or how to argue back until I learned the words. Once I understood what was happening and why, in terms of institutionalized racism and so forth, I was able to fight back, or at least channel my anger into more productive routes than angry, speechless flailing because I couldn't coherently reply.

"Learning race theory and sociolinguistics was empowering," she finishes.

Deeper understanding, confidence in her experiences, and a sprinkling of anger fueled Helen towards political activism on campus. "I had a strong sense of justice and injustice," she states. Rather than sitting quietly, Helen felt she had developed a vocabulary and knowledge base at camp that she could now put to work. In her freshman year of college, because of the social justice issues brought up in camp, she joined a group that was concerned about Michigan University ending its affirmative action policy. She gathered her courage to fly to D.C., rallied at Georgetown University, and marched in front of the Supreme Court. From there she discovered a strong group of women in the Asian American Student Union (AASU), women who wanted to educate, mentor, and politicize other young women at the college. Helen explains, "I spent most of my time listening to people who are more politically aware and articulate about issues."

Then she did a semester in Beijing and spent time confronting her "American-ness" versus her "Chinese-ness or "Asian-ness." Yet when she returned to Scripps, she found that suddenly "I sounded like I knew what I was talking about." Laughing, Helen imagines her fellow students responding, "Wow, Helen has good ideas! She's worth listening to! That's so strange!

"I could articulate my ideas, challenge myself and others," Helen states. She went on to volunteer in New Orleans after the floods. She became an advocate for the disenfranchised communities there, particularly people of color. Helen muses, "A lot of people in college were a lot of talk but no action." But here she was becoming the change she wanted to see in the world, and she's happy to share the story of her journey with others. She wants to show that apathy or dissembling are not her style. "I don't feel ashamed about anything I have to say," she notes.

"It's empowering to others to know that real people are sharing their stories," Helen says. "So many Asians and Asian Americans are seen as passive or apolitical. If I hadn't gone to camp, I would never have gone to D.C., never met the amazing women there who got me into the AASU. I likely would not have met other amazing women of color or the queer students group.

"Camp changed me," Helen continues, leaning forward. "It started me on the road to being politicized, to realizing that the personal is political, and that the political is personal. It opened up my brain, so that I realized that yes, one person can cause change; it's lots of people coming together thinking that together we can cause change, and it made me brave enough to want to speak up."

At camp, Helen had seen beyond the mahogany skin, the accent, or the dreadlocks. "I saw people as people, not their race," she asserts. "They were really good people, whether they were loud, hyper, or cool. They came out of their shell." So did Helen, which was the most empowering change of all.

Second Time Stuck

The thin sophomore sat shivering under a blue fleece blanket, looking paler than usual, her straight dark hair hanging loosely to frame her face. Even though Shereen was right in front of the blazing campfire that our "pyros" had stoked, she still felt chilled as she pulled her body into a ball.

"Are you okay?" her friend Valerie asked her, her brows converging.

Through chattering teeth Shereen replied, "I'm so cold!"

All around her, other campers perched on the damp logs that formed a square close to the campfire, their songbooks open on their laps. Others sat on the wooden bleachers further back, watching the fire's sparks rising up into the redwood branches above. They laughed and put their arms over each other's shoulders and swayed in unison to songs like "Imagine" and "I Believe I Can Fly."

By the time we finished singing "Stand by Me," Shereen had thrown off the blanket as beads of sweat popped out on her forehead. "Now I'm burning up!" she told Valerie, who in turn went to find Michael, my colleague and partner in organizing our trip to camp.

"Can I call my dad?" Shereen asked Michael once he had been located and brought to where she hunkered down miserably. "I'm feeling really awful. I want to go home."

"Of course," Michael replied, and they went off to call home and pack Shereen's things. It was Friday night, and two full days of camp had passed, though Shereen would miss out on the culminating activities of the final day.

Shereen had been a shy freshman, never raising her hand in geography class and only fraternizing with her close friends. She wasn't a risk-taker. That reticence was one of the reasons that her geography teacher Tracy had recommended she go to camp. "It's an experience, Shereen," Tracy had said encouragingly. "You should try it." At camp Shereen had continued to stick with her small circle of buddies, laughing with them, but not making much effort to get to know the other delegates.

However, there were a lot of stereotypes against camp that Shereen had had to overcome, and she had signed up for camp despite what others had told her about it. Around campus, there were rumors. "I heard everyone will hug you," Shereen recalls, her brown eyes going wide. "I heard that they make you cry at camp. People said it's a waste of my time, that camp is for pussies." These comments generally came from students who had never attended camp and got only snatches of information because delegates are asked to keep camp experiences confidential; campers can talk about their feelings and what they learned, but we ask that they don't disclose private information or tell the details about the activities so that future delegates will have a purer experience untainted by false expectations.

Though Shereen had heard some negative remarks, she trusted her teacher's word. Besides, a couple of her friends that she wanted to hang out with were going to camp. "But what if I'm separated from you guys?" she had said to Valerie on the bus ride through the mountains. "Who will be in my cabin? What are we going to do there?"

Valerie had smiled serenely, tilted back her head, and replied, "You should just give it a try."

Once Shereen had arrived at camp, she had had even more misgivings. When she saw where she'd be sleeping on a worn, wooden bed frame with a striped, plastic mattress, she was afraid to lay out her sleeping bag. "I want my nice, clean bed at home!" she wailed, looking to her cabin mates for support. The pale linoleum floor, the open wooden beams, and the flimsy yellow curtains didn't provide any more comfort.

At dinner that night, Shereen heard the others' comments. "There's a whole salad bar!" Ashley exclaimed.

"Have you tasted the chicken and gravy?" Derek asked. "And look, someone's putting out chocolate pie for dessert!"

Shereen just bit her tongue and poked at her food.

"I'm kind of in over my head," she thought later as she left camp, though she still felt disappointed to be heading home.

Shereen ended up with the worst flu of her life and spent the next five days in bed. However, in spite of her doubts about camp, something about it had touched a chord inside her. She recalls, "I learned to be more accepting of others, and I learned a lot about different cultures at camp."

After giving it more thought, she continues, "I think the things we learned at camp should be brought back to campus to make the school environment much better and bring more people together versus keeping the cliques together. Everyone is the same, and no one is better than others." She became a regular at Wednesday club meetings, where camp delegates and supporters gathered to have ice cream socials, fund-raisers, and movie nights to discuss controversial films. She was often one of the first to arrive at events, usually with Valerie, and she began taking on little jobs, like keeping attendance. "I'll help make posters," she'd offer, her hand upraised. She always made a point of greeting people, and I grew to rely on her to take care of things when asked. My first impression of her was that she looked anemic, but I saw a vibrancy grow in her as the year went on, and she always had that ready smile.

The following fall, Michael and I held interviews with potential student counselors. We were selecting students who would be designated Counselors-in-Training or CITs to help facilitate small group discussions and lead ice breaker games or provide other leadership roles at camp. Ours was one of the few schools that had successfully recruited and utilized CITs, and we felt a responsibility to choose the most highly qualified applicants.

I was surprised when Shereen signed up for an interview. Though she had been so solid in the club all year, I remembered that she had left camp early due to the flu. Had it really been illness? I wondered. Or had she gotten too nervous or homesick and needed to escape? Had it been a case of her being too shy and self-conscious, too young, to open herself to the emotional risks that camp might necessitate?

But the past year, Shereen had proven that she was responsible and followed through with given tasks. In her interview, she talked about how she had learned not to be judgmental of others. "I'm more open and willing to accept others," she told us. "I don't judge others by their race; I don't accept the stereotypes." Here was a young woman who had been so quiet and now was forging a clearer identity. She went on, "It's okay to be different, to be an individual. My heritage makes me unique. People say I'm an interesting mix." Shereen told us more about family gatherings where she made big pots of pasta like her Italian grandmother did, yet her mother's side spoke Farsi at home and were brought up Muslim. As she grew up, she learned about Ramadan and celebrated Persian New Year. "I'm extremely white, as anyone can see," she said, "but I'm also Persian. It all plays in to who I am. With all the backlash against Muslims or the problems with the Middle East, I have to talk about that with people, but I'll laugh and joke with people, too."

Shereen's poise impressed us, and we chose her

along with nine other students to return as CITs. "The second time, I was ready for everything that happened," says Shereen.

During gender empowerment night, Shereen was really touched. "It let me see what boys go through," she remembers. "Yeah, a lot of people cried, but it's not like everyone cries. It's just a really intense experience, and a lot of people really let their feelings out." At camp Shereen's second year, she also saw how gender night affected some of her friends who were there with their boyfriends. Shereen hadn't done any dating yet, declaring that she hadn't met anyone intriguing enough, but seeing what others went through gave her the vicarious experience. "If you go to camp with your boyfriend, you get to learn all this stuff about him and get to know each other better," she says.

One of her new friends, Krissy, disclosed past abuse on that night, and Shereen witnessed how Krissy's boyfriend Bobby supported her, not just with hand holding and hugs, but with unconditional emotional support. Seeing Krissy's pain, Bobby wanted to protect her and also help her deal with how this disclosure would affect Krissy's family.

Furthermore, Shereen was able to see the vulnerability and suffering boys experienced due to stereotypes that society supported. Many of the young men held in their feelings or had trouble expressing their pain, and they shared what they had been through as well as what they felt during the gender empowerment exercise. "I'm more appreciative of what each gender goes through or contributes to life and what I can learn from them," Shereen concluded. As a CIT, she also got to facilitate further discussions, helping boys as well as girls debrief the activity and continue to work through their feelings. "I think the second time was different because I was a leader, and I wanted the new people to experience things in a positive way," she concludes.

Since Shereen had gone home early from her first camp, she had missed out on Saturday's forced segregation activity. But at her second camp, she participated with the Middle Eastern students, a small group consisting of only three delegates, one of them Shereen's younger sister. Richard had instructed all participants, "You must stay with your group at all times, and you can't talk to or make eye contact with members of the other groups."

When her group visited the bathrooms, she saw the signs we had posted for the "whites only" and "colored only" toilet and sink. "I was so shocked that this is how it was in the past between blacks and whites," she recalls feeling. "I saw all the hate. People are so mean when they're dealing with people who aren't their race." But back in the main hall, as she saw her friends separated into groups labeled "Asian," "Latino," "African American," "Jewish," "White," and so on, she realized that past history wasn't so far in the past. Similar kinds of prejudice were happening today, only with every group, not just blacks and whites. Remembering that morning, she tells me vehemently, "It wasn't right. I wanted it to stop right then and there, for it to be over with."

Though Shereen experienced these shocks and

insights, she realizes that her learning from camp happened gradually, as a culmination of the many activities. "It taught me different things at different times," she feels. Perhaps one of the biggest changes was the shedding of her shy self. She describes herself now: "I'm really loud now and goofy all the time. I don't really worry what other people think of me." To get over her shyness, she learned at camp how to make friends. "I used some of the camp tricks to get to know people," she says with a grin, "like not judging people based on their looks but taking the time to get to know them. I'm more willing to talk to people besides just my friends," Shereen says, and I think back to that reticent girl who went to camp because her friends were going. Shereen's teacher had described her as a person who never took risks, but that had changed. It's said that the most successful people are those who take risks, who step out of their comfort zones and try new things.

Shereen gives another tip for making friends. "I try to be their friend first, even if they don't seem to want to be my friend." She sticks by people and finds ways to make them comfortable, to laugh, and this is a skill she uses now constantly as she works her way through college and babysitting jobs. "When you go into the workforce, you'll have to work with many kinds of people," she realizes, "and you have to get along with all of them. So camp is a really great experience to prepare for that.

"The second time I went to camp," Shereen realizes, "I reminded myself of what I had learned the first time. Going the second time really made it stick. I got to help other students learn what I had learned, so the lessons stuck better." Before I could even ask her if she felt that everyone needed to attend camp twice for real learning to endure, Shereen was quick to add, "But it was also my choice to make it stick in my life. I wanted to keep it."

Bet You a Nickel

"I don't know if I should've come to camp," Matthew confided to Laura, his art teacher who had signed up for camp as a counselor. Laura's so approachable for students, in her open manner and casual, often paint or clay spattered clothes, that kids know she's willing to talk about things and better yet, to listen. Matthew and Laura stood in the slanting, late afternoon sunshine by the sand volleyball pit as the new arrivals descended from the school bus and surveyed their surroundings.

"What's going on?" Laura asked as she and Matthew scrabbled through the lumps of luggage for his duffle bag.

"I'm not sure this is the place for me," Matthew replied. This oversized, pale boy hung his head. "I mean, everyone seems to have friends, and people are hugging. Did someone say there's going to be sing-a-longs?" he finished with a pained look. This was a long string of words for a young man who spoke little in class. He had arrived at camp knowing only a couple people, and he held himself apart, keeping his eyes down and his hands in his pockets. Laura had been worried about him falling into the wrong crowd of kids back at school. Now she noticed that most kids getting off the bus were clumped together with the people who looked like them—black kids with black kids, Asians together, nerds on the fringes away from the athletes in the middle of the crowd. It was a common scene when students first arrived at camp.

Laura put her hands on her hips and got Matthew to look her in the eye. "Matthew, stick it out. I have a feeling you'll be happy you came. I'll even bet you a nickel."

"A nickel? Okay," he replied, and they shook on it.

Laura first decided to go to camp when she was a new teacher at her current high school. She had been teaching at an alternative high school and before that had been a group home counselor, often parenting teens more than teaching them academic content. She had helped countless kids deal with unintended pregnancies, drug and alcohol abuse, running away, criminal records, abusive parents—you name it, she had seen it in kids terribly battered and self-protective and still only teenagers. She had been called a bitch or told "I hate you" by angry, battered, self-protective teens more times than she could recall, yet here she was ready to sign up for a camp where she knew potent emotions would surface, where people were pushed out of their comfort zones. It was like volunteering for a hurricane.

"There was a presentation at a staff meeting at school," Laura remembers. "Camp sounded interesting. In the presentation, there were students who had gone to camp and talked about their experiences. We also did an exercise like something they would do at camp."

Laura cocks her head to one side and pulls her long, curly hair off her neck. "It was an intense little exercise," she says, "but it didn't scare me off. I thought this staff was interesting, and I hoped to get to know them at camp."

Before the students had arrived at camp that Wednesday afternoon, Laura had participated in the staff training. In the morning, they sat at long, white plastic tables in the chilly main hall, dishing up scrambled eggs, toast, and bacon. "Hang on, camp is quite a ride!" a returning staff member smilingly warned her.

Susan, another counselor, must have noticed Laura's raised eyebrows. "Don't worry," she reassured Laura. "You'll be fine."

"Now I feel more nervous than before," thought Laura. She felt wary and didn't want to let her guard down with simplified reassurances, even though her years working at a group home had equipped her to deal with strong emotions.

Susan and Laura bused their dishes and went to help others set the green plastic chairs into a circle, creating that screechy metal-on-linoleum sound as twenty chairs were dragged around. The room was warming up, but cups of coffee or mocha helped, too. Staff training would last about six hours, before delegates arrived in the afternoon.

"We'll start with a getting-to-know-you activity," Richard explained to the staff seated in the circle. Staff may include parents, teachers, or other school staff, such as administrators, counselors, the health clerk, and even students as CITs. We also usually have a police officer and other community members hired to be counselors. A couple CITs passed out white folders and handouts to everyone. Laura wrote her name on her folder, crossed her legs, and immediately began doodling a lizard, her artist side emerging.

Richard leaned forward, elbows on knees, and continued, "We'll also go over camp norms, how to facilitate discussions, and the schedule of activities."

"I'm a quarter Arabic, the rest Caucasian," Laura explained later in the training, during one team-building activity, "and my parents named me after the donkey they rode in the Grand Canyon." Her smile was part playful, part smirking, her dark eyes twinkling. The training helped build trust and comfort levels amongst the staff while also modeling the activities they would later use with delegates.

However, the next evening's gender and sexism discussions put everyone to the test. "The stand up/sit down part of the activity visually brought home for me how many women and girls are victims of harassment and violence," Laura recalls. This is the activity where Richard reads a list of statements that the women stand for if something applies to them. Statements range from restricted choices, such as not going places alone at night, to inequality, name-calling, and physical violence.

"Some of the issues that the men stood for overlapped the women's, but I also really got it for the first time, how often boys are pressured to be tough, not cry, not show feelings, not care, be strong, be assertive, be protectors, be physically powerful," Laura remembers, her voice impassioned. She had noticed Matthew in the crowd, seemingly paralyzed in his turmoil of emotions. "I realized that these things become a recipe for disaster when we stir them together with women who have been raised to be subservient, unassertive, afraid, and insecure about their self-worth. We end up with gender roles that make it difficult and often dangerous to get along. I think for women, it is easy to place the blame for this at the feet of men, but men are victims of this, too. These things plague our society. This activity gave me a great deal of compassion for what men go through in our society," she finishes.

Moreover, during Laura's first year at camp, over fifteen students disclosed that they had been abused or molested, and Laura, as a mandated reporter (as all teachers are), helped with the reports to Child Protective Services. "That year was the first time I did that exercise," Laura recounts, "and it happened to be an incredibly intense year where a lot of things came up for a lot of students. It was really heavy." We've never had that many disclosures or reports before or since.

Delegates had been carrying these secrets and burdens all alone until they had this opportunity to disclose to someone else and begin a process of finding safety or healing old wounds. Numerous students seek counseling or police intervention, or they open dialogue with people who have hurt them, such as friends, family, or boyfriends and girlfriends. Laura is one of those teachers who students know will listen and help them find their way.

In fact, when Laura thinks of her most powerful moments at camp, they're really about the delegates, not her own growth. Speaking of her first time experiencing the gender empowerment activity, Laura states, "Seeing the growth and changes that can happen in a three-hour window of time—it was really powerful that you could have that kind of change." Laura looks off to the side for a moment before continuing. "This is the stuff that's really important to them and that they want to talk about. These are students who often have a difficult time focusing through a fifty-minute math or history class, and here they are sitting for three hours at a stretch on hard plastic chairs. They're engaged because they're grappling with all these issues.

"There are so many students who are incredibly brave," Laura adds, "who would speak up even though they knew it would make them angry or make them cry. There are students who are obviously empathic and are kind and nurturing to the kids who are hurting." She continues, tilting her head, "The students always amaze me. I just watch them transform, be willing to take risks, stand up for what they believe in, admit that they made mistakes in the past." Laura remembers a student who used to carelessly throw around terms against gays. He saw her on campus after camp and proudly yelled, "Hey Ms. Rice, I haven't said 'That's gay' in six months!"

Laura states, "Definitely a part of the camp experience I like is having those students in my class the rest of the year as allies." When a new student enrolls in her art class, Laura can pull aside a camper and request, "Would you make sure the new student feels welcome? Show her around the room and sit with her this week."

"You got it, Ms. Rice."

When she's demonstrating a new project, like making sand mandalas, she might privately ask, "Hey Amy, when I introduce this mandala thing, I need you to be really enthusiastic and get the other kids excited about it. You can ask the other campers, too. Can you do that for me?"

"No problem."

"Often campers do things without my asking, like jumping up to clean the spilled paint," Laura adds, her voice rising in surprise. After their shared experience at camp, these students are often so open and willing, enthusiastic and kind. "I know I can trust them," Laura shares. "They get it."

Laura naturally focuses on the changes she sees happening with the students, but what about the ways camp has affected her? "As a teacher I was more willing from that point on to take more risks in terms of my lesson plans, the kinds of things I would incorporate into those classroom activities," she explains. "I teach art, but we do a lot of lessons that address issues like bullying and stereotypes, privilege and family relationships."

For example, early in the year Laura wants to set the tone for her classroom and let students know what perspective she is coming from. She begins, "Today we are taking a break from art. You have the option to not participate," she explains, though she finds that virtually all students do. Laura has students write a list of the ten things most important to them based on their personal life philosophy or religion. Is it love? Kindness? Family? Not being judgmental? Each student gets to read one thing from his or her list aloud. The students always come up with great lists that include things like being a good friend, working hard, having compassion, and being kind and loving.

Then Laura connects this exercise to the issue of homophobia. "When faced with situations like discovering their classmate is gay or lesbian, so many students forget their lists of what's important to them," Laura says. Next, Laura hands out cards containing true statements by gay, lesbian, bisexual, and transgender youth. The cards say things like, "My dad found out I was gay, and he beat me and kicked me out of the house."

"It's really shocking for kids to hear these cards," Laura comments. "They sit really quietly and hear all the cards, then talk about their list of values." Laura asks students, "What are we doing to create an atmosphere in our school that promotes so much fear that a gay student is twice as likely to commit suicide? Is this what we value and what we want our community to promote?" Laura ends the lesson by providing definitions of terms, resources for more information, and even advice for different situations. "Kids ask, 'What do I do if my friend comes to me and says he's gay?'" Together they brainstorm options and answers. "I don't want to tell them what to believe," Laura explains. "I just want them to make sure that their actions and their words match their lists that they created at the beginning of class." After this lesson, Laura notices a dramatic decrease in homophobic remarks in her classes.

At camp, delegates also learn empathy and communication skills when they role play intervention strategies or when the small discussion groups talk about taking the lessons of camp back to their friends and families. Over the years, a number of delegates have come out at camp, disclosing their sexual orientation or simply feeling comfortable enough to be themselves. Laura engenders that comfort both in her classroom and at camp.

Not surprisingly, the largest number of kids signing up for camp come from Laura's classes.

Laura may know that she can implicitly trust her camp kids, but they know they can trust her, too. Kids confide in her all the time, from the ones who wait by her door every morning to the quiet ones like Matthew who may only answer when she prompts them. It's no exaggeration that her intervention has saved the lives of numerous kids. Yet for Laura, "It's not a big choice; it's just the right thing to do."

After going to five camps, Laura understands that some students aren't quite ready to accept its new ideas or take in all the emotions that are stirred up. "Even the students who are quiet or seem really timid or not willing to share out loud," Laura explains, "I think they all come away with a great experience. I think some of them aren't ready to talk but that the learning still happens."

There's a Buddhist saying, "When the student is ready, the teacher appears." For some delegates, they may remember their camp experiences a few months or even years later, when they find themselves faced with a crisis or in a racist situation, and then the words they heard at camp will bubble up as from some deep well to provide the guidance that they need. Laura adds,

"There have been some students who have gone to camp that I thought were vulnerable or fragile in some way but who have benefited greatly from their camp experience. A lot of them are stronger than we realize."

The "Forty Developmental Assets" research by the Search Institute shows that particular skills help children to become successful adults. Camp promotes growth in so many of these areas, such as increasing communication skills, building empathy, showing kids that adults in their community care, seeking equality and social justice, and helping kids work with people from different cultural backgrounds. Training for counselors fosters these skills, and certainly, Laura has incorporated these assets into her classroom as well, such as promoting a safe and caring school climate.

At the end of her first camp, Laura wanted to make sure she found Matthew in the crowd. Delegates were piling back onto the bus in a rainbow of races—Latinos hugging Asians, white kids calling out to black kids, gays chatting with straights. Kids were slinging their sleeping bags into the bus' hold, others were snapping last-minute photos or signing each other's white camp t-shirts. Laura searched the fringes of the crowd for that tall boy with the sandy brown hair and kind eyes.

Laura found him helping a girl with her ponderous suitcase. "So do I owe you a nickel?" she asked him.

"Naw," Matthew replied, smiling wryly, "you can keep the nickel."

I Got My Billy Back

"Did you see that kid with the little red ball?"

"Why does he keep bouncing it against the wall?"

"I don't know. He's kinda weird."

"Have you talked to him?"

"No, he doesn't talk to anyone. He just bounces that ball all the time."

"I can't see his face because of that raggedy, old, brown hat he's wearing."

"Yeah, what is he, a cowboy?"

"I don't know. But he keeps making these creepy grunting noises, too."

"What's his name?"

"Billy."

That was Wednesday, the first day of a three-and-a-half day camp. Surrounded by ninety campers, Billy was still alone. It was the same in my classroom; Billy was always isolated. A lot of it he orchestrated by burying his head in a sci-fi book or, at camp, engrossing himself in bouncing his red handball. Sometimes a student would make a friendly overture just to be startled when Billy suddenly shook himself and snorted like a horse. People quickly found a reason to leave him alone.

"I was used to being shunned, being an outcast,"

he says.

And yet, for all that aloofness, Billy had signed up wanting to come to camp, a place where he knew he'd be expected to interact with a large group of people. He'd have to talk about stereotyping and prejudice, when all he usually wanted to talk about were video games and sci-fi novels. On campus, he so immersed himself in books that he even ran on the track during P.E. with a fat paperback in his face. He sometimes sneered at other students in class or made dismissive remarks about them, such as, "Video games? Yeah, you wouldn't know about that." Occasionally he reveled in a maniacal laugh, eyes big, hands like claws, making others wonder if he had done something gruesome. Why would Billy choose to go somewhere where he'd have to bunk with others and talk to them all day? "I just wanted to get out of my classes for a couple days," Billy admitted, shrugging. "It sounded interesting." Yet somehow I knew there must be a different Billy inside just yearning to break out because he often stayed after class to talk to me about the things he loved. He seemed hungry for contact and someone to listen to him.

Billy's mom had informed me, over the course of numerous emails and phone calls when he was in my freshman English class, that Billy had had a difficult past. Due to problems with his mom's boyfriend at the time, her four kids had been taken from their mother just before Billy was to start third grade. They were put in foster care, then got bounced from shelter to foster home to group home for a couple years. The shelter's school wasn't very good, so Billy had had to repeat third grade. His mother finally got custody of two of the kids again when Billy was in fifth grade. She whispered intimations of abuse and molestation in foster care, though Billy never spoke of it, even when I asked him directly. "I don't really remember much about the foster homes," Billy admits, putting his hand to his chin and peering upwards. "I think I got kicked out of one. I kind of lost track of time." Billy's mom started carrying a sheaf of papers about Billy's learning disabilities and her various custody battles, like a shield to help her protect her children.

The statistics on foster care are alarming. According to the California Department of Social Services' website, about three-quarters of children in the nation receiving foster care are there due to neglect. On average, children stay in foster care for about two years and often have two to three placements. The majority of children will reunite with their families, as Billy did, yet their futures still remain bleak. About seventy-five percent of foster children work below grade level at school, and forty-six percent don't complete high school. In a situation exacerbated by Billy's group home placement, no one had identified his learning disability until his sophomore year of high school, which, coupled with his social isolation, contributed to his numerous failing grades, despite the fact that he scored well above grade level on reading comprehension tests.

The website Adoption.com reports that nearly half of former foster children receive counseling or medication for emotional problems. This fit Billy's profile, too; he had been happily engaged in counseling for a few years, and he spoke openly of its efficacy. But without intervention, what might the future hold? Adoption.com also discloses that after leaving high school, half the former foster children remain unemployed, and twenty-seven percent of young men will be incarcerated within twelve to eighteen months. Could this be Billy's fate? Or might his little sister end up as one of the nineteen percent of young women who will have unintended pregnancies? Between ten and twenty-five percent of foster children will become homeless. Certainly, there are lasting effects for children who experience separation from their families, and without further counseling or intervention, many of these children don't receive the skills or support they need to be independent and successful, including the positive self-esteem that can result from a loving, stable home.

During the months before he went to camp, Billy had acted out often in my class: saying rude things to others, never turning in his homework or not doing class work, or completely ignoring everything that went on in class while his head was buried in yet another book about aliens. These were probably coping methods he had learned in the group homes and various schools he had attended. In contrast to the ninth grader I knew, as a kid Billy had been so friendly and outgoing that his mom had had to teach him not to talk to strangers so easily. With a laugh Billy recalls, "I learned to ask their names first so they were no longer strangers!" He loved to talk to others that much. However, a few years of foster care had knocked that friendliness out of him, creating the social outcast I had known when he was in ninth grade.

Billy had learned to be a loner to protect himself. He wore his funky, dark-brown leather hat that flopped into his eyes, shaggy yellow hair peeking out over his pale skin, and he sat in self-imposed exile.

Until camp started to work its magic on him.

Billy's discussion group leader was Mike, the über-parent, who had had over eighty foster kids come through his home. Tall Mike, with his ever-present camouflage pants and ubiquitous smile, had the patience and open heart to reach Billy. Mike simply loved kids, whether they were babies or teens, shy or gregarious or weird. This small discussion group listened to Billy and drew him out. "They told me that it was really great talking with me," Billy tells me later, his eyes widening. They'd start a topic, and Billy would lose himself in the flow of it, until he discovered that his previous self was returning, the self from before foster care and isolation. First it was questions about himself.

"How are you unique?" Mike asked the delegates in his group.

"Well," Billy quipped, "I carry this red ball with me everywhere. And I can read a book in a day," he added brightly. "The last book I read was over eight hundred pages." Billy trotted out the safe and familiar topics of books and video games.

Next the small discussion group moved on to questions about friends and leadership. Grant, the CIT, asked, "How are you a leader? How can you influence the behavior of others?"

Billy shifted somewhat uncomfortably at these

questions, but he still spoke up. "I can try to talk to people, I guess," he hazarded in reply. "I can tell them what I learned at camp."

But soon, instead of always throwing his red ball against the wall, Billy began simply holding it in his hands during group time. Then others started incorporating him and his ball into games; the ping pong players paddled his ball when playing with him, or he'd be seen tossing it to kids on the swings. He was included into the campfire circle because he loved helping with the fire, setting up the logs or staunching the embers, and then others drew him up to stand during singing time. The privilege activity opened his eyes. Billy noticed, "People can seem one way, but then I found out that their lives had gone a completely different way," he said, his hands gesturing their movement away. Maybe he saw that his life could go a completely different way, too.

That was Thursday.

By Friday, the next-to-last day of camp, Derek, another CIT, asked, "Billy, where's your ball?" Or someone offered, "Billy, come play cards with us." Or another asked him, "So what are you reading now?" When Billy went off by himself, Grant always seemed to find him to bring him back into the fold. "Billy!" Grant would call like he'd found a long-lost friend, then put his arm around Billy's shoulder.

The ball pretty much disappeared.

Billy's face grew ever more animated, his eyes brightened, and his words began to flow.

In fact, it became difficult to shut him up. As his

discussion group talked about family, Billy spoke more openly about his mother and siblings, particularly his little sister. "My mom got custody of my sister Christie again, but she can't get my other brother and sister back," Billy confided, his voice growing softer. "We think they're being brainwashed against my mom." Then his voice grew stronger, vehement, as he talked about his dad. "My dad's a racist," Billy spat out. "Especially after being at camp, I can see that clearly. I loathe that." Those discussion sessions, he says, brought him back to his old self and taught him new things about himself that he wouldn't have grasped on his own. "I realized I shouldn't judge people," Billy states in retrospect. "I should get to know them and find out new things about them. I have a new view of the world."

Pretty soon, Billy babbled on energetically and avidly. By Saturday afternoon, as we were putting kids onto the bus to take them home, I was not the only one willing to be cornered into a conversation to have the pleasure of seeing this hermit crab emerge from his shell. Mike listened because he had enough room in his heart for a million foster kids. Derek thrived on helping people grow. Grant just liked an audience. "People told me that it was great talking to me," Billy recalls brightly.

After camp, once we had returned kids to their families, I heard from Billy's mom. The English department phone rang, and I immediately recognized her voice.

"What did you do to Billy at camp?" she asked, while I momentarily panicked that she was criticizing the program. Oh no, I thought, Billy's done something terrible or told his mom that we brainwashed him or made him do things he didn't want to do. Maybe he got home and broke down crying. But instead I had to smile when she said, "I got my Billy back."

A Capaciousness of the Soul

"A Santa Clara University education promotes a capaciousness of the soul," intoned the priest during the commencement ceremony invocation at Buckshaw Stadium. He went on to speak of the university's ideals of intellectual freedom and especially service, that the university graduated individuals who would go on to positively affect their communities. Hundreds of black-gowned students sat under the blazing Saturday sun patiently waiting to officially graduate. I could see poking up at the back of the group the spikes of Chris' mohawk where he anxiously fidgeted, awaiting that moment where he could cross the stage and receive his diploma.

Swallows zipped and dove over the proud families who craned their necks to pick their loved ones out of the crowd. When it was Chris' turn to cross the stage, it was easy to spot him as the only grad not wearing a mortar board hat, his four-inch blond-tipped brown mohawk cutting through the crowd like a saw blade, his black tassel hanging from his right ear. He often pumped his fist in the air and looked back at the crowd to see where his friends and family sat laughing (or maybe cringing).

As with any graduate, it had been a long road for Chris to reach this point, but in his case a more remarkable road considering he had been expelled from his high school in the ninth grade, the year he was my student.

Nevertheless, Chris was an engaging, charming, unique character. Moved by boundless, fidgety energy, he never sat still. I suppose he could be a teacher's worst nightmare, but I admired his huge enthusiasm for his passions, and I relished his unique take on the world. When we had Socratic-style discussions in class, Chris would get a new idea, sit up straight in his chair, open wide his eyes, raise his arm like a flagpole, and bounce in his seat until it was his turn to talk. He wasn't one to interrupt others, but it was like trying to contain a stampede. Chris was also a good listener, leaning in towards people, swallowing every thought, asking questions—perhaps so he could use these ideas in his own argument, but it still made for spirited debate.

And Chris had a sharp mind; it was not by mistake that he had been placed in honors English. He had an immense spirit barely contained in his thin frame, and that spirit burst out in ways both delightful as well as inappropriate for the school setting, yet those were some of the things I admired most in him: his questioning of the status quo, his refusal to merely accept the rules without wanting to know why they existed. "At school, I hung out at the hill where various people met up," Chris recalls, "where cliques melted together. Punks, preppy kids, skaters—the clique barriers got broken down."

Engaging, challenging, that was Chris, and sometimes he went too far. Still, his expulsion had come as a shock. That incident had taken place eight years before on a field quite different from the graduation ground. Students were dressed in period costumes for the annual Renaissance Faire put on by the ninth grade accelerated English classes. Colorful booths lined the edges of the field, with students selling headdresses, jewelry, candles, and more, while maidens prepared for the Maypole dance, and jousters waited by the Queen's stage. That year, students had set up stocks next to the stage; at one point I, one of their teachers, had been locked into the stocks while a student humorously sold me to the highest bidder in a mock auction. And I wasn't the only one; another of the presiding teachers had also been coerced to put her head and hands between the wooden slats. Yet what began as fun became the opportunity for a stupid decision, one that changed Chris' life.

Chris saw someone leaned over, locked into the stocks, and viewed it as an opportunity he couldn't resist. "This butt was there, and my friends were all watching. I thought it'd be funny to whack it, but I didn't know what to use. Then I thought of my shoe," Chris remembers. Not even knowing it was a teacher he had struck, he then cupped his hand around her chin and said, "Don't worry, honey, it's not so bad." That patronizing act was perhaps worse than the anonymous blow with a shoe, recalls the teacher, for it carried all the self-assurance of a male who thought he had the right to dominate a female. The public nature of the event made it that much more denigrating and humiliating for a teacher to be thus treated in front of hundreds of students, especially a new teacher still establishing her credibility at the school, not to mention that she was trapped in the stocks, at the mercy of others. Though that teacher is a good-natured and fair-minded person, it was clear to everyone present that Chris had crossed a line. He was admittedly being a dumb fifteen-year-old boy who ended up getting expelled for the remainder of the school year on the grounds of sexual harassment. At that point, Chris really had no clue as to the gravity of the incident.

In the aftermath, I talked to Chris' mom a number of times. I already knew her quite well from previous incidents that year, such as the time Chris turned in a poetry project with song lyrics full of violence, profanity, and misogyny. I had dreaded having to make that call; I really did love that kid, and it's not that I didn't think that his parents deserved to know what kind of work he had turned in or that he didn't deserve a reprimand, but I was so hopeful that he would do the right thing instead of something dumb. I didn't want to be disappointed in him or, for that matter, to see his very conscientious and respectable parents' frustration arise once again.

Chris is one for pushing limits—and pushing buttons. His nickname is a perfect example. Chris' mom is Japanese-American while his dad has Polish roots, which resulted in Chris' light olive skin tone, tall and thin frame, and light eyes, with a faint Asian slant to them. In elementary school, when kids encountered Chris, they'd be confused and ask, "Are you from China?" The nickname "China" stuck. I was horrified that Chris would embrace this name that was at once racist and also denied his actual heritage. Everyone called him China, but it always stuck in my throat.

After Chris was expelled in April of his freshman year, I dreaded that this punishment would send him down a discouraged and bitter path where he might take out his anger on The System by choosing to fail, or he might figure that since he was in trouble already, why not create more? I wrote a letter on his behalf to bring him back to our school for his sophomore year, and then I got him to go to camp. Chris remembers, "I had heard about it from friends and was curious. I was ready to have a life-saving experience."

Chris recalls the nervous energy he felt upon arriving at camp and the anticipation of big things to come. "There were a lot of cool, open-minded people. We stayed up the first night talking in our cabin," he recalls. The eight young men and their adult counselor lay in their sleeping bags after "lights out" and kept talking into the wee hours. "Everyone got along, forgetting all the groups they always hung around with. All those clique barriers in high school were already disappearing," Chris recalls.

Gender empowerment night was the turning point for Chris. When he saw the girls in tears, when he heard the stereotypes against his own gender, and when he realized the power that these gender roles had to affect others' self-worth and life experiences, he had his epiphany.

"I never want to use my gender to demean and disempower anyone ever again," he emphatically states now. "I can still remember the tears coming out of people's eyes." It wasn't only the tears and hurt of gender night that he wanted to assuage; it was the years of societal mores that had led him to strike a woman in a vulnerable position that he wanted to understand in order to undo the wrongs and change things for future men and women. "Being socialized as a male and having no idea of what privilege you have as a white male, you don't know what impact you actually have. You call someone a fag or a bitch and don't know how it affects people," Chris says.

As he continues, his thoughts spill out from an internalized pool. He speaks with an impressive confidence and knowledge. "On race and gender nights, I realized there's some crazy shit that goes on in our society regarding how people are treated as second-class citizens due to their gender or ethnicity. There are things we can't control that we're born with, and we have a whole different life experience because of it." Chris admits, "My whole goal to work for social justice came out of those two nights. Now I try to work towards equality and not perpetuate the race, class, and gender stereotypes and power structures."

Furthermore, Chris was tested at camp. On gender empowerment night, our Assistant Principal showed up in support of the program. This was the man who had insisted on Chris' expulsion, Chris explains. "I remember sitting next to him and thinking, 'I hate you so much.'" Rebecca, a CIT, helped Chris calm down. "I didn't want to bring my own crap into it," Chris confesses about that night. He was able to contain those feelings and even gave the man a hug at the end of the evening.

Rebecca and others helped Chris deal with so much. He explains, "Camp can help you find a great support group. They can back you up. Especially in high school, you're just starting to find yourself, and kids can be evil when they're insecure." Chris left camp with a whole new circle of friends.

Chris is a hugely empathic person, a quality he layers over with things like raucous music, profanity, and humor. But when a moment requires him to be real, he's immediately there. Pain stays with him—primarily the pain he's caused others; in fact, when he talks about that fateful day at the Ren. Faire, he still breaks out in a sweat. Every day that he had to pass the room of the teacher he had struck, he recalls, "I put my head down and hoped she didn't see me." He's never quite gotten up the nerve for a face-to-face apology, though he wrote her one after the incident.

But that memory of pain became a prime motivator directing Chris' path. For his junior year of high school, Chris took the American Studies program, in which students did weekly public service and reflected often about its role in society and their lives. This program gave him the chance to volunteer in his community and further clarified his goal to work for the betterment of society. His senior year, Chris went on to be a CIT at camp, well-loved for his playfulness and easy-going manner, and well-respected for his ability to be a confidante and listener. "Take it easy, man, it's all good," might be his response after he's just listened to someone's troubles and offered insightful and helpful comments.

Chris' mom confided in me that she wasn't sure he would make it through high school, yet he graduated with the grades to be accepted into Santa Clara University to major in Psychology and minor in—here's the kicker—women's and gender studies. Being the only man in his program gave him a unique perspective to contribute as well as a powerful opportunity to learn from women. Was he still trying to make up for that woman he had degraded at the Renaissance Faire?

"I may still have those traits and habits from my upbringing, but I have more awareness of it now," Chris admits. His voice becomes serious as he zeroes in on his ideas. "I watch my own behavior and try not to contribute to the oppression and disempowerment of other people."

When asked what lesson he took away from camp, Chris characteristically replies, "The skill to not be an asshole." He may laugh as he says this, but the earnest desire to do the right thing is obvious in his comment.

If Santa Clara University's mission is to produce "leaders of competence, conscience, and compassion" as stated on the university's webside scu.edu, then these three traits meet in Chris. That "capaciousness of the soul" is his, and I have no doubt that he'll go on to be an engaged member of his community as the university hopes for its graduates. Chris' education had begun back at that Renaissance Faire eight years before, had become focused at camp, and had led him to the degree he had just attained.

"Can't I just stay a kid a while longer?" Chris asked in a small voice. "I'm scared." But underneath that fear, or that bravado of a mohawk at graduation, lies a young man sincerely wanting to do good in the world. When asked what else he has to say about his camp experience, Chris yells an enthusiastic "Thank you!"

For More Information...

Silicon Valley Faces
777 North First Street, Suite 220
San Jose, CA 95112
408-286-9663
www.svccj.org

About the Author

Kathleen Ann González started out as a teacher but was surprised to find that she was a writer, photographer, and dancer as well. While she spends most of the year trying to infect teenagers with her great enthusiasm for literature, she still squeezes in time to write about her work and her travels. Her first book, *Free Gondola Ride*, is about the gondoliers of Venice, and she has published several essays and articles over the years.